P9-CAB-630

Endorsements

"With raw honesty and great courage, Michele tells her redemptive story so that we might find hope and freedom to step into God's purpose for our life. Well done, Michele."

— RUTH GRAHAM
author of *Fear Not Tomorrow, God Is Already There*

"If you think for a moment that you have out-sinned God's forgiveness, meet Michele's Savior. With startling clarity and heart-jolting honesty, Michele's story is a stunning window of hope. It's time to step out of our musty hiding places and join this brave, broken, redeemed woman in the light."

— PATSY CLAIRMONT
Women of Faith speaker and author of *Kaleidoscope*

"*Untangled* reads like watching a great movie. I was sorry when it ended. Michele's is a deep, rich, pain-and-glory redemption story. A beauty queen, a harsh childhood, solace under a bed, a beautiful voice. *Untangled* is universal and unique. I lost myself in it and found myself at the end standing on the Rock."

—VICTORIA JACKSON
actor, writer, and comedian featured
on *Saturday Night Live*

"Thanks, Michele, for leading me safely home with your story."
— BEBE WINANS
multiple Grammy and Dove
award-winning recording artist

"Some will describe this as an autobiography; others will call it a true-to-life mini novel. To me it will forever be a scalpel in the hand of God. *Untangled* did surgery on me."
— ALLEN SHAMBLIN
Hall of Fame Songwriter: 2011 Song of the Year CMA, AMA, and Grammy for "The House That Built Me"

"*Untangled* is a story of redemption told with beautiful transparent stories that boldly reveal Michele's journey of life to her readers. I love her already! I am thankful for women like Michele who are willing to share the messiness they have endured, ultimately shining a bright light on the Lord's grace, mercy, and love through their testimonies."
— SHARI RIGBY
director, author, actress, and speaker

"For everyone who feels like Humpty Dumpty after the fall, my dear friend Michele Pillar has a message for you: The king's horses and men never had the power to do anything. It's only the King who can put you back together again. With unusual honesty and candor, Michele allows you a peek into her messy life so we may better see ourselves. *Untangled* is a mirror image of you and me, and a vivid reminder of the marvel of redemption."
— JOE BATTAGLIA
president, Renaissance Communications,
and author of *The Politically Incorrect Jesus*

"*Untangled* is nothing short of an act of bravery. With a deft pen, Michele allows readers into the hidden, vulnerable places of her life's story—including both glorious joys and bone-crushing pain. But she doesn't stop there. Michele goes on to write the anecdote for the secrets that have bound us, and how we can truly live without shame. Don't miss this book!"

— ALLISON ALLEN
author, speaker, and actor (Broadway, Women of Faith)

"Michele Pillar writes from the heart and lays out a blueprint for untangling our emotions. We have all felt stuck and trapped, like there was no way out. Michele has been there and did find a way through with God. She comes to us with a banner of hope and promises of redemption in *Untangled*."

— MARGARET PHILLIPS, MS
licensed marital and family therapist

"I was accosted by Michele's honesty."

— TIM MARSHALL
Vice President of Distribution, Word International

"*Untangled* grabbed me from page one and wouldn't let me go!"

— LISA PATTON
author of *Whistlin' Dixie in a Nor'Easter*

"You will be surprised at the backstory of this pioneering Christian artist. Michele writes with amazing transparency and honesty. Darkness gives way to light. God meets her where she is, a true message of grace."

— DR. LINDA MINTLE
speaker, BeliefNet blogger, and author of *Letting Go of Worry*

"*Untangled* is sacred. It is the incarnate Word of God fleshed out in the life of a modern-day woman, a woman whose heart and mind (perhaps like yours and mine), knotted through childhood circumstances, is touched by the gentle hands of her Savior— Jesus, bringing beauty from ashes, gladness from mourning, praise from fainting, freedom from prisons in her mind and heart. We all have things to untangle in our lives. God's heart's desire is to help us become untangled!"

— LEORA SHANKS
educator

"She dances a jig on a thread of sheer courage, laughing in the face of adversity. I never once felt sorry for her and in fact I envied her journey. Bravo, Michele!"

— GARY KELLER
CEO of Keller Williams International and *New York Times* bestselling author of *The Millionaire Real Estate Agent*

"She's untangled! Without it, she NEVER could have written this book. If you feel tangled up in anything, read and find freedom! Grace Chapel will be using *Untangled* in our home groups."

— PASTOR STEVE BERGER
Grace Chapel, Leiper's Fork, Tennessee

MICHELE PILLAR

UNTANGLED

THE TRUTH
will set you
FREE

BroadStreet
PUBLISHING

BroadStreet Publishing Group, LLC
Racine, Wisconsin, USA
BroadStreetPublishing.com

UNTANGLED: The Truth Will Set You Free

Copyright © 2016 Michele Pillar

ISBN-13: 978-1-4245-5294-8 (softcover)
ISBN-13: 978-1-4245-5295-5 (e-book)

All rights reserved. No part of this book may be reproduced in any form, except for brief quotations in printed reviews, without permission in writing from the publisher.

Unless otherwise noted, Scripture quotations are taken from the Holy Bible, New International Version®, NIV®. Copyright ©1973, 1978, 1984, 2011 by Biblica, Inc.® Used by permission. All rights reserved worldwide. www.zondervan.com. Scripture marked NKJV is taken from the New King James Version®. Copyright © 1982 by Thomas Nelson. Used by permission. All rights reserved.

Stock or custom editions of BroadStreet Publishing titles may be purchased in bulk for educational, business, ministry, fundraising, or sales promotional use. For information, please e-mail info@broadstreetpublishing.com.

Back cover photo by David Bean
Front cover photography by Meggie Low Velasco, meggie.low.velasco@gmail.com
Cover and interior design by Michele Pillar and Meggie Low Velasco
Interior typeset by Katherine Lloyd, The DESK

Printed in the United States of America
16 17 18 19 20 5 4 3 2 1

Dedicated to the Beautiful *One*

Contents

FOREWORD BY DUSTY WELLS. 13

1 YOU CAN'T FRIGHTEN THE DEAD. 15

2 THE BEAUTY OF A TOP SHEET 33

3 THE POWER OF FORGIVENESS. 41

4 FOUND 55

5 EATING CROW AND KEEPING IT DOWN 73

6 IN SEARCH OF THE INVISIBLE MAN 91

7 RALPH. 105

8 WOMEN AND ROSES. 119

9 SAVING FACE 125

10 THAT'S WHY I NEED HER 139

11 LIVING IN THE LAND OF OS 147

NOTES 168
ABOUT THE AUTHOR. 169
MORE FROM MICHELE PILLAR 170-175

"*Untangled* is written inside out and out of order because that's how God found me and because restoration surprises us at unexpected moments and in impossible situations."

—Michele Pillar

Foreword

The music industry is full of amazing stories and songs of hope, joy, love, and peace. So many great artists and writers share through song about life, love, and all the other mysteries we, the listeners, get to enjoy. The beauty of music is that it deeply touches a part of our heart that nothing else can.

But rarely, if ever, do we get to look into the beautiful full restoration of someone who as a young, successful Christian artist disappeared and then resurfaced, healed and restored. Very few times do we have the chance to experience and understand what went on beneath the surface, when no one but God was there with that artist.

Now, my precious, longtime friend, Michele Pillar, has done just that—with courage, grace, and hope written into every paragraph. She's back! She's been back for some time now, with a fresh new message of encouragement and restoration and how God, in all of His greatness, never left her side.

In this book, Michele writes about life with a fresh, bold depth of conviction, sincerity, apology, sensitivity, and vulnerability very few have chosen to write about. She will take you on a journey you won't soon forget! She has made the choice to dig deep into her own past, failures, struggles, and issues, thus bringing them into the open, and in doing so, not only helping herself, but helping the rest of us who are struggling to become *Untangled*. Michele's cinematic stories will give many people, who are in the midst of desperation, trying so hard to move beyond the wounds of their own past, *hope*! And for those of you who have already found resolve, you will celebrate with her!

In chapter one, Michele opens with such power and visual detail, I could feel her heart pounding, I could smell and taste her desperation, as I read each word. I was tempted to stop reading, but I'm glad I didn't!

What I love even more about this book is that Michele candidly laughs about it all now, and *that* is helping so many who have at one time or another lost their way or feel so endlessly alone in their earthly journey with God.

Michele has always been beautiful to listen to, but she has something more to say here, and I want to listen even more so to it. My friends, I invite you to sit down in your favorite quiet place and take some time to listen as well.

Michele is opening up her heart and soul to you, and I guarantee, her openness will help you in whatever it is you are dealing with.

—Dusty Wells
Senior Director, Sales and Marketing,
Word Entertainment

Chapter 1

YOU CAN'T FRIGHTEN THE DEAD
untangling the knot of hopelessness

Year: 1985 / **Age:** 30
Place: mom's house in the converted garage

"You've been nipping at my heels my whole life! I can't outrun you anymore. Go ahead; show me what you've got. Get it over with. Finish me off!" In my mind I was yelling at him at the top of my lungs, but in reality my pleas were barely audible. There was no need for a gag over my mouth or twine as a ligature. He knew it, and so did I, too exhausted now to move, too weak to scream.

The object of my disdain was standing strong and steadfast right in front of me but not close enough for me to take a swing at. Any hope of escape was way out of reach as well. In fact, any hope at all was laughable at this point. He could have leaned in, pressed his nose against mine and breathed his foul breath down the front of my neck, and I'd have let him do it. I'd taken guff from him all my life. At one time I had a strong kick. As a kid, I learned how to punch and scratch my way out of his filthy hands and got pretty good at ignoring the manic voices in my head. But now my arms felt like lead; so did my legs, soul, and spirit.

I'd never been able to see his face before now—only his handiwork. My life was riddled with it. Considering everything that led up to this moment, it was no surprise he was here and crystal clear in all his ungodly glory. It made perfect sense.

With my mind working in 20/20, it was a relief to finally put a face on the one who'd caused me so much pain. He was as real as the dirt on the floor and the mold in the air. Questioning his validity was a moot point now. An ugly smirk was stretched across his even uglier face. He was leaning against the far wall like he was holding it up. He reeked of self-confidence. His arms were folded Indian-style across his rail-thin chest. His legs were crossed, too, with his right foot resting atop his left one. His body language spoke sheer satisfaction.

My words felt feeble yet were somehow sharp and to the point with the intent of egging him on. I wasn't kidding. The whole thing needed to end this night, one way or another. I wanted more from this guy than the idle threats I'd put up with forever; I wanted him to make his move.

With my head in my hands I asked myself over and over again, "How on Earth did I get here? How did I get back to this hellhole of a house I grew up in?"

I was sitting on the edge of the twin bed I'd hidden under as a child and remembered how this rickety thing had once been a friend to me: a safe, dark place of refuge. Whenever my parents went on a full-fledged binge, or just threw back a couple of vodka tonics, our tiny house backslid into a five-alarm meltdown. I was well versed at reading everyone like a book. And thank God for long legs that winged me to safety more times than I could count.

When the yelling and screaming hit the three-quarter mark,

my mother would take off down the hall, headed straight for the coat closet. That's where she kept her implements of torture—an ample supply of unoccupied wire hangers. Her trail of bobbing, weaving, and bumping against the walls as she went knocked our family photos right off their nails. One by one they hit the wood floor, and glass shattered everywhere. As each frame broke into a million pieces, it was as if that family member was shouting out Mom's exact location to me. They always helped me, letting me know just how much longer I had to find a hiding place. By the time she slammed open the closet door and fished out one of those thin, nasty hangers, I was safe and sound, hiding under my dear friend of a twin bed. I'd fling myself under it and lie on my tummy, quiet as a mouse. With my heart pounding in my ears, it was hard for me to hear where she was. But her shouts of "Michele! Where are you?" always gave her away.

That's when I did all I could do—pray. I prayed it the same way every single time. "God, please don't let anything happen to me." Before I could say "Amen," a peace covered me like a blanket. This is my first memory of God. Our family didn't go to church, so God came to me. He found me under that bed. He met me there every time. My mother never thought to look under it. Not once. Sad to say, I didn't always make it to my bed on time, but when I did, God made me invisible.

But what was I thinking? If not for the bruisings, did I really need to hide? Most times my mom and dad were so engrossed in their own insanity there was no need to worry about little ole' me. I could have plopped down on the sofa and watched it all play out like a tennis match on quaaludes, and they wouldn't have noticed me sitting there. But I ran anyway, afraid of the crossfire. Heavy objects were known to fly without warning. Or

I ran because I thought I was somehow to blame. Now that I think about it, any little person nearby could be pulled into the line of reasoning, without cause or notice. And there would be no correct answers in that interrogation. Since I was the youngest of four girls, I was an easy target. My sisters always fled, except for Madeline. If she was around at the time, she protected me. If not, I was left behind to face the music alone. I was too young to run away from home, so I ran up . . . up the stairs and straight to where God lived, under my unmade bed.

But now at thirty years of age, finding myself back here sitting on this pee-stained mattress didn't feel anything like a sanctuary to me. I was eighteen when I left this house the first time. My newfound faith in Jesus carried me far, far away from here. Since that time, I'd owned my own home a couple of times over, had a booming career as a Christian recording artist, enjoying all the trappings that came with it. Just eight miles up the road and two blocks from the Pacific Ocean stood a sweet cottage with the names Mr. and Mrs. Pillar on the mailbox. Two ancient avocado trees stood strong and tall in our backyard and gave us more guacamole than we could eat. We had friends—too many to count—and a faith that seemed strong and true.

So, what on Earth could have driven me back to this house of shame and torment? My guilt-ridden mother wasn't asking for details yet. She'd been down this road before, welcoming back any of my three older sisters when their lives fell apart. I'd always thought I was different than they were. I never believed I'd have a reason to return to this awful place.

But "never" came a'callin'. A few nights earlier I packed a small bag and drove away from my life in Huntington Beach. I watched my pretty little cottage fade to black in the rearview mirror of my late model Volvo.

Could I have grabbed a nice hotel room instead? Or better still, could I have afforded a furnished apartment to think things over? Certainly.

But the deep feeling of shame and grief over what I'd done to annihilate my marriage covered me like a shroud from head to toe. The sting of disappointment with myself and of disappointing God told me I wasn't deserving of a respectable place of comfort. After leaving my husband, going someplace clean and nice didn't dawn on me. At the time, I didn't understand why I moved back here. But now I realize that, in order to pay penance, I marched straight back to the only place I felt I deserved. This, the house I grew up in.

The phone was silent. The friends were gone. The husband was angry, reeling and out there covering his tracks against me. And it hurt, but I understood. I'd messed up. Big time. And losing everything—my marriage, my ministry, and every friend—all at once was more than I could take; so earlier in the day I purchased an extra-large bottle of sleeping pills and was fully ready to swallow every single one of them.

The only friend that showed up to my going-away party was the horrid creature, the father of lies, standing in the far corner of my old bedroom. I wasn't asleep. This wasn't a nightmare. It was as if I was dreaming—wide-awake. I'd never been one to drink—not with alcoholics scattered throughout my family tree. I'd never been one to take pills. I'd never smoked anything. I wasn't attracted to the paranormal and didn't have a tendency to blame Satan for my troubles, but I may have underestimated him.

I wasn't hallucinating. I wasn't alone. This cinematic showoff's performance was bigger than life—mine anyway. This was personal and with a specific goal in mind. Yet, if any outside observer had stumbled into the room, they would have seen nothing but a girl sitting on a bed at the end of her rope. But in my mind, it was all loud and clear. Maybe it was just every low-life, insecure thought about myself I'd ever had, manifesting as a twisted daydream. Or maybe it was the not-flesh-and-blood warfare the Bible tells us we fight against every single day. Either way, in this my darkest hour, darkness himself showed up in living black and hideous.

I could feel what he felt. He stood immovable, dressed in his full regalia, something that's both impossible to explain and impossible to forget. The God-forsaken creature pointed his long, bony finger at me, began laughing hysterically, and answered my "How did I get here?" question with, "Who did you think you were anyway?" He elevated his craggy voice to a shout. *"You thought you could leave here?!"* He threw his head back and howled at the moon that was just coming out to play. "You can't leave this house; you ARE this house! Everything about it runs through your pathetic little veins! Where's your Jesus, your so-called savior, now? You've traveled the world doin' your thing for him!" He smiled and took a second to reload the hole in his face, "You gave him your youth, you gave him your voice, and *for what?*"

The demon laughed again and again and taunted, "You thought you could dress up like a Christian and convince the world that you're better than all this?"

His eyes slowly surveyed the dilapidated filth I inhabited, but then snapped back at me. "You gave your god everything. Where is HE now? You're right back where you started, little girl. You didn't get anywhere! You'll never get anywhere!"

I believed him. Every single word of it.

He was saying everything I'd been thinking, everything that had driven me back to this house. I just sat there, looking down at the cracked linoleum floor, nodding my head over and over in agreement with him. I felt like I had a cannonball-sized hole in my soul. I didn't have an ounce of kick left in me. I wasn't the slightest bit afraid of him or the situation. That's how I knew I was already dead. Under normal circumstances I would have been scared to death, but you can't frighten the dead. That's how I felt—dead. That's what I wanted to be—dead. I was too tired to feel or fear anything and too spent to have dreamt this all up. Every failure, every fear of success, every rotten and lonely day I'd ever known paled in comparison to this one. I was so tired of expecting more out of myself than I could deliver.

"You're right!" I told the thing. "You're absolutely right." I said it again and again. My voice softened, and I asked him, begged and pleaded with him, "Please, just help me do this. Let's just do this . . . okay?" I whispered. I so hoped this *deus ex machina* could come through for me. I'd fought this house my whole life and everything it stood for. I couldn't come back here, yet I hadn't the strength to go anywhere else.

The "how did I get here?" question kept racing through my mind. The sun was setting, and I didn't kick on the lamp. For the first time in my life I couldn't hear God's voice. I couldn't feel one ounce of God around me or inside of me.

I'd served Him, taught thousands of people about His abilities, powers, love, and forgiveness. But He didn't seem to be anywhere near me now. Only months ago my life looked as though it was in order. Now all I could picture were bowling pins standing upright; then, without warning, they were crashing at random, as the heavier-than-they-are bowling ball hit them with such force that there's nothing they could do but go flying—hitting walls, hitting each other, then falling silent.

The quiet was like nothing I'd ever known.

For years I had a schedule that was impossible to meet. Interviews, more than I could fulfill. Even now there were concert dates on the books I'd have to carry out with people like the Billy Graham Association, Oral Roberts University, and Houston First Baptist Church. Limos and town cars took me anywhere I needed to go. Family and friends helped out by doing things I didn't have time for, like laundry, reading boxes of fan mail, even helping me shop for clothes to wear to the next big event.

I ate out 99 percent of the time and then had to work out at the gym at least four days a week to wear a size four. At five foot nine, that's nothing less than unrelenting slavery. I traveled from city to city two hundred days a year. Only months before, I'd been on the Grammy Awards telecast in front of millions of people. Michael Jackson wore a glove on one hand, while I was dressed in a classic Halston gown. Both Annie Lennox and Cindy Lauper told me during the show that I seemed "different" from the others. I was thankful Jesus was there guiding me, shining in His own gentlemanly fashion. I truly felt called of God to carry His light wherever I went, and I loved doing it. This calling possessed me from the first moment I asked Him into my heart in 1973.

I'd worked hard to fulfill every request anyone asked of me. The president of the record company told me I was the hardest working artist he'd ever signed to the label. And, yes, I enjoyed the accolades that followed. These pats on the back were perks for a little girl who grew up in emotionally and spiritually bankrupt surroundings. A girl who, when she found Jesus, found the Father she'd never had.

What else was there for her to sing about? What else mattered? What else was more important than Jesus? I had no choice. I wanted no other. I hit the highways and byways at the age of nineteen, when contemporary christian music was but an embryo. I—and artists like the 2nd Chapter of Acts, Keith Green, and Phil Keaggy—sang in church basements from the bottom of our hearts. The Maranatha! Music praise albums were just beginning, and little did I know the solos I sang with braces on my teeth would one day be deemed classics and would out-live me. Amy Grant was still in high school and was listening to the LP Erick Nelson and I recorded for Maranatha! called *The Misfit*. We sang for pennies and never thought to ask for more. Lives were being changed, and so were ours.

At first I thought I could keep up the pace. I felt powerful and authentic. But as time passed, I was elevated higher than my roots could steady me—up, up, up on a spiritual tightrope. I found it difficult to believe my own press, because it was larger than life and running on ahead of me. I eventually knew that one good gust of wind would blow me off the rope, and I'd topple to the ground. Yet, at the same time, I thought I could do anything in Jesus' name. My motto was "He is strong in my weakness." He was so amazing in what He did through me! I just kept praying that my essence could catch up with my public image.

But now, sitting on this bed, I couldn't lift my head from my hands. I wondered if the real truth was I'd been running on my own steam the whole time? Running to get away from this house or just running from myself, really. Was Jesus real? Or did I make the whole thing up?

The only logical thing to do was to take my own life, because there seemed to be nothing of value left of me. In self-detonating my marriage, I ruined my reputation as a minister of the gospel. Local stores caught wind of the gossip and pulled my music from their shelves. None of them called me to ask the validity of the rumors. It was just as well they didn't. I wouldn't have had the strength to answer their calls. And the worst part was, I had absolutely no idea why I'd done what I'd done.

Why such a knee-jerk move? I asked myself. *I mean, an affair, Michele. Really? What an idiot. You are beyond disgusting.* I condemned myself. I thought surely God felt the same about me. Surely He walked away, too, and for the same reason everyone else did. They tiptoed away, truthfully. They left in disgust. I was not pleasing to them now. I was not productive any longer. I was a liability, a disappointment, and an embarrassment. I was disgusted with myself and wanted to walk away from me too.

So tonight I would walk away from me.

Today I was on the cover of *Today's Christian Woman Magazine*; tomorrow I'd be known as the Christian singer who copped out and killed herself.

In 1 Samuel 5:1, King Saul's public image was more important to him than anything else. He didn't take the time to build the inner strength necessary to lead the people. This deceptive road led him to tragedy, the taking of his own life. We humans are all alike; no matter what century we live in, we tend to gravitate toward shortcuts. Even though I started out serving God with vim and vigor, spiritual sloth had lulled me to sleep and straight back to this horrid house.

My pseudo-support system of managers, booking agents, and assistants was long gone. This demon was the only one managing me now, encouraging me to go ahead and do exactly what King Saul had done. In my mind, my suicide was a foregone conclusion.

The sun was fully set now. The room was pitch-black, and this darkness was heavier than any I'd ever known. My make-it-or-break-it moment was now. There was nothing more to talk about.

I lifted my head, stared down the demon, and said, "Go ahead, take me out."

Looking at the pills and imagining how they'd feel going down my throat, I thought about my mom and how sad she'd be. With one last glance back in time, I thought of the letters. There had been a dramatic change in the fan mail over the past few months. Instead of writing and asking for an autographed photo or a specific recording, now people were expressing concern. Over and over they said they were praying for me. "Are you all right?" was the question scribed on page after page by countless people. The letters were frantic in nature, and they apologized for asking such personal questions. Yet their concerns wouldn't let them not ask. The letters made me nervous. The authors seemed to know more about my future than I did.

I rolled the pills around and around in my hand. "Did God send His people ahead to fight for me, knowing this night would come?" I considered the idea.

"None of that matters now, Michele." The enemy pressed, persistent.

I closed my eyes, placed the first pill in my mouth, and whispered, "I don't want this, but there's no other way."

I sat still, stalling, fighting with myself. Feeling the air going in and out of my lungs, hearing my heart beating its last beats with the bitter taste of death in my mouth. With eyes clenched shut, I dug deep down inside hoping to find one more ounce of courage.

Then, without warning, someone sat down next to me. The person's depression in the mattress shocked me. I gasped, embarrassed, or the way you would feel if someone shook you from a deep sleep.

Who knows I'm here . . . like this? I thought. Adrenaline shot through me like lightning.

Whoever it was sat down so close to me you couldn't have slid a playing card between us.

I opened my eyes.

It was Jesus. His hands were clasped together. He was leaning forward, His elbows resting on the tops of His thighs. He wasn't looking at me. His eyes were fixed on that demon still standing across the room.

Jesus was as still as stone.

It was as if He was waiting for something, but for what, I didn't have a clue.

Silent and fixed, I gazed at Him with no desire to look anywhere else. His face was the most beautiful face I'd ever seen, yet not by human standards. My face, on the other hand, was burning from too many tears. He straightened up and gently put His arm around my shoulders. I tucked myself under His arm. He was as real and touchable as the vile creature had been. That dark presence, by the way, was long gone. The Light sitting beside me had swallowed it up. There was no space left in the room for anything or anyone else but us.

How my mind's eye saw all this so clearly, I can't fully explain; I only know it took place when my life was hanging in the balance, and this was how God fought for me. He allowed me to see a glimpse of how dark darkness is. Then He let me see Him, that He was bigger than my choices. He was bigger than my darkness and my mistakes. I am—and forever will be—grateful.

I had confessed Jesus as my Savior thirteen years earlier. I'm sure He looked beyond my first prayer to this moment. He knew that this would be the day I'd need a Savior. As I look back, I see that God (although in total disagreement with my choices) was not ruffled, rattled, or repulsed by me because of my choices, any of them. The blood of Jesus was my camouflage to the Father. No other covering or cleansing is an equal advocate. Even while I sat there with dirty hair and with mascara running down my cheeks, guilty from head to toe, to Him I was His bride dressed in spotless white! This clear photograph of God's perfect love for me will never fade from my memory or tarnish with time.

I spat out the pill that was melting in my mouth. Then I opened the empty bottle and dropped my life back inside the plastic container, one pill at a time.

God meets helpless people every day who have no time to spare, no time to pray, no time to make it right, as when driving on frozen bridges and ice-paved roads at midnight. He wraps His arms around the chest of the doe just as she's ready to leap in front of our cars. He stands with us when we're crumpled next to a hospital bed praying for our loved ones, or when we're on the gurney ourselves. And when we stand over a casket we never dreamed we'd stand over, He stands beside us. And yet again, the night our spouse leaves us, never to return, Jesus is there—when we feel Him and when we don't.

The next thing I saw during this encounter was a ball of string. I looked down, and in my lap sat a large, very tangled ball of tiny threads, the size of a basketball. The threads that made the sphere were knotted beyond what anyone could or would try to untangle. It made me think of the time I found a fourteen-karat gold chain in the bottom of my jewelry chest, tangled beyond its worth, so I threw it away. That's what I wanted to do with my life, but God had much different plans.

Jesus looked down at the ball of string, then looked me straight in the eye. *Michele, give Me your life.*

I smiled a smile soaked in tears. "I did that years ago. It didn't work for me. I am so sorry," I answered in apology.

He repeated Himself, *Give Me your life, Michele. I want the whole thing.*

I knew what He was asking for, but He explained it to me anyway. *I want every part of you. The parts you've never given Me, the parts you've hidden. The ones that were Mine that you gave away and the ones stolen from you. Even the parts you don't know how to give Me, I want it all. There are pieces of your life, like the threads in this tangled mass, I've never been allowed to touch, to untangle, to change, to heal. There are crimps buried beneath threads, and because you can't see them, you pretend they don't exist. The knots and snags in your life are holding you back, catching you off guard, and keeping you from becoming all I designed and created you to be. It's time to give Me the whole thing, to give Me your whole life.*

He took my hands and placed one on top and the other underneath the ball of string and continued. *There is work to be done. We'll do whatever it takes to release and untangle each knot.*

He unwrapped me from His loving grasp and placed His hands on top of mine and said something I will never forget. *I could untangle them, all of them with one touch, but you wouldn't know how they got tangled to begin with and would walk out of here and tangle them all again. So, I am asking you to work together with Me until every last thread is free. There is wisdom, knowledge, and healing at the end of every knot. For the first time in your life, I want to show you the true definition of grace. I'm giving you back the parts of your life that are yours to keep track of and yet ours to take care of. You'll do your part, and I'll do Mine. Some of them are the tender threads of your youth, taken from you when you were too weak to hold on to them. Together we will reclaim and rebuild what is rightfully yours. It will take a lifetime, Michele.*

I sat still and in amazement. Nothing had ever been made so clear to me. It felt so good to feel my life in my hands again.

And in His. The life I'd lost somewhere along the way. The life I almost threw away. Yes, it was tangled, but for the first time, I didn't care about that. I had it back. My tangled life was right where it belonged, safe in between God's hands and mine.

I asked Jesus, "Will we be staying here in this house the whole time?"

He smiled. *You don't belong to this house. You are not this house. You are Mine, Michele. In time you will walk out of here, never to return.*

Then we just sat together. Quiet.

He said, *Always remember. Remember this, Michele. Remember us.*

"How could I forget You? You're the only One I know. The only One I have. The only One who came here. Well, You and that . . . thing."

Then I cried.

Jesus rested His chin on the crown of my head, wrapped His arms around my heaving shoulders, and let me cry. I cried in thankfulness, in regret, and alas, I cried in sweet relief. There seemed to be a plan. A plan for a future and maybe even for His glory. But the only thing that mattered now was that He was with me and would stay, no matter what. I'd really never known that before. Not until now. Maybe all that had happened could somehow matter. Maybe my life could finally stop hurting.

When I had no more tears to cry, I collapsed into my pillow and tried to get some sleep. The battle was over. New life could begin.

Every detail of this encounter is as clear in my mind today as it was when it happened in 1985. Just like those who see Jesus while on operating tables and in ambulances, I saw Him.

Jesus came to me. He saved my life that night.

Was I "saved" before that time? I thought so. I spoke to Him, lived for Him. I sang about Him all over the world. But did I really know Him and trust Him? And did He know me? This is the question I wonder about to this day. I'm not 100 percent certain of the answer. Thankfully, it doesn't matter now.

This I know. I needed to know the Jesus who sat beside me on my bed. I needed to be certain He knew me, all of me. The devils know who He is and they tremble.[1] This makes me think of the sad story when Jesus said to the person at the threshold of eternity, "I never knew you; depart from Me."[2]

That person called Him Lord and had done miracles in His name. Yet somehow, Jesus didn't know him. I scared myself when I behaved in 1985 as if I'd never known Jesus, holding sleeping pills in the palm of my hand. At best, I was dancing on the edge of grace. At worst, He did not know me yet. Although I was doing many things in His name before that time, I don't think I was doing the will of Jesus' Father.[3] When someone like me looks and talks like a Christian, yet does something out of the blue and completely off the wall, as I did, you have to wonder if they have taken full responsibility for their end of the bargain as a follower of Christ.

I wonder what would have happened to me if I had swallowed those pills that night? How tragic for me if I'd found myself reasoning with Jesus as a stranger like the man in the book of Matthew did.

The security of my relationship with Him rests in His promises, but the depth of our relationship rests with me—spending time with Him, getting to know Him, enjoying His love, and giving that love away. Serving Him plays a part, but service alone is not enough. I know that now.

I lived in my mother's house for the next two years, sleeping like a baby in that twin bed, telling Jesus my truths and watching Him reveal how one thread was connected to the next one. Sometimes I just listened, and I began understanding things about myself and about the choices I had made. I devoured the Bible with eyes that didn't shy away from the hard truths it wanted to teach me. I pressed into the pain and allowed God's words to do everything they're intended to do. He and I untangled knot after knot together. We are still doing that. Some threads are stubborn and complicated, don't want to let go. Others give up without a fight, yielding with a gentle tug. And so the sphere gets smaller every day.

I no longer pretend to the world that I'm more than I am, because I know who is sitting next to me. I know that showing people my flaws doesn't in any way dilute or diminish Jesus' beauty and power. My flaws don't change who He is. My flaws don't lessen His love for me. Jesus is the Beautiful One *in spite of* my knots and *for the sake of* my knots. And He sees me as beautiful, and so I'm learning to do the same. He didn't see me as broken that night in '85. He saw me as broken open, and that's the most beautiful broken of all. And as for my mask, the one I wore trying to be beautiful? Well, it's gone. It shattered into bits at the feet of my Lord that night. I threw it away instead of my life. I knew something needed to go, and God knew exactly what it was.

Chapter 2

THE BEAUTY OF A TOP SHEET
untangling the knot of insecurity

Year: 1964 / **Age:** 9
Place: my house and Dee Dee's house

ee Dee knocked on my front door and rubbed the grimy glass with the sleeve of her Barbie T-shirt. Flakes of ancient paint snagged her shirt and floated down to the cracked cement stoop. Still, she couldn't see anyone inside, so she opened the door and poked her head in. "Can Michele come out and play?"

Neither my mom nor Janeen got up from the kitchen table, though Mom glanced up from her *Look* magazine and yelled, "Come on in, Diane. She's up in her room. Just follow the sound of the screaming Beatles and the rumble of her pounding feet, ready to come through the floor any minute! You can't miss 'er."

There they sat, where they always sat—my mom and Dee Dee's mom, Janeen—both nursing beers and smoking Virginia Slims like they were going out of style. It was somehow comforting to me—the surety of it. I could find Mom in that same chair every day at 3:15 p.m. when I got home from school. That was one of the few things in life I could count on.

On this particular day, Janeen brought Mom last month's *Look* magazine. The cover was a warm, evening-time photograph of the White House, decorated with holiday trim. The issue had a sticker slapped across the intended title, "Christmas at the White House," that now read, "In Memory of John F. Kennedy." It featured "A Christmas Message," written by Jackie Kennedy prior to the assassination of her husband and closed with the instructional article, "How to Run a Household." I doubt Mama read that one. The never-ending pile of dirty laundry in front of the washer was proof of that.

But to her credit, Mama never afforded herself things like *Look* magazines and didn't keep weekly hair appointments at the beauty shop as most women did. Everything she wore came from the sale rack at Zody's Discount Store, yet she always found a way to provide us girls with multivitamins in the morning and Country Club Malt Liquor for Janeen and her in the afternoon. I think the *Look* was offered in trade.

My best friend, Diane René Bass, a.k.a. Dee Dee, scaled the dirt-stained wooden stairs, three at a time, to find me cuttin' a rug to the number-one radio smash in the United States, "I Wanna Hold Your Hand." The LP had hit stores the day before, and I was at the Rusty Needle when their doors opened at 10:00 a.m. The tiny record store was in Garden Grove, nine miles from my house. I rode my bike for what seemed like forever with my babysitting money stuffed in my left shoe. The shopping bag carrying the precious LP dangled from my handlebars and got tangled in the spokes three times on my way home. The first time it happened, I swerved and skinned my elbow on a cinder block wall. The second time I veered into oncoming traffic, trying to right myself. But thank God, the LP survived the trip, and that's all that mattered to me.

"Hey, Dee Dee! Aren't they groovy?"

I was munchin' on a bag of plain M&Ms, something I rarely did. I never had a big sweet tooth, to Dee Dee's delight. She always got to finish off whatever sugary thing I was eating at the time. At birthday parties, she asked for the corner piece of cake with the frosting rose perched on top. I always asked for a piece from the center, no rose, and I scraped off most of my icing and gave it to Dee Dee. She liked the whites of the egg, and I preferred the yolk. We were a match made in heaven! And she lived right next door to me.

I raised the small bag of candy over my head and twirled under it as if it were Paul McCartney's hand holding mine.

"Here! Catch!" I said and tossed her the bag. It ricocheted off the ceiling and split wide open. The colorful orbs went flying everywhere. Dee Dee hit the floor and scrambled on her hands and knees, plucking them up before they got squished beneath my dancing feet. Oblivious to her efforts, I mash-potatoed over her right pinkie finger.

"Owww! Hold the phone, Michele!" Dee Dee begged.

I stopped, closed my eyes, and cupped my hands in midair pretending I was holding Paul's face close to mine, "And when I touch you I feel happy"—2, 3—"inside"—2—3—4—1, "It's such I feeling that, my love," (kick drum fill), "I can't hide, I can't hide, I can't hide!" I sang to my imaginary boyfriend at the top of my lungs.

Dee Dee rolled her eyes but kept on task, risking life and limb, stuffing her face full of the little confections as fast as she could go. On task, too, I kicked high on beat four, and a red M&M went flying. Dee Dee missed the catch, and the ruby morsel rolled under my bed.

I winked at her. "That one's for God!" I shouted.

Dee Dee disapproved, "Nuh-uh!" and dove under the bed, skinning her back on the metal bed frame.

I stopped dancing. "No, really, Dee Dee, leave it be!" I demanded. I yanked on her T-shirt, ripping the lace trim. "Dee Dee, I'm not kidding. It stays under there," I said in monotone. When she refused to listen, I grabbed her by the ankles, pulled hard, and she bonked her chin on the floor.

"Dang-it, Michele!"

Dee Dee was kneeling on my pee-soaked PJ bottoms from the night before, so she slid out from under there without any trouble. She stood to her feet, pressed her lip with the back of her front teeth, and covered her mouth. I leaned in and pulled her hand away to assess the damage. She shoved me across the room. The Beatles skipped all the way to song number four. I lunged at her but stopped myself short of socking her in the belly. Instead, I pulled her hand away from her mouth again and saw nothing more than a split lip, oozing blood. I was relieved. There was no trace of a red candy shell.

"You and that God-under-the-bed thing are stupid, Michele." I didn't say anything back.

I went over to the record player and gently picked up the needle and turned the machine off. I slipped the shiny record back in its cardboard sleeve, trying not to scratch it, and said, "Let's just go over to your house, okay?"

"Sure," Dee Dee answered. She grabbed the last few M&Ms and popped them in her mouth, leaving the red one under the bed. We headed downstairs and next door.

That was the first time I can remember defending God. Not that He needed me to. Or maybe I was defending my faith in Him. It would be eight more years before I'd know Him by name or crack open a Bible. Words like *born again* and *salvation* were nowhere to be found in my vocabulary. I didn't know Easter for anything more than chocolate eggs and black patent leather Mary Janes that pinched my toes and blistered my heels. But this one thing I knew: God was real, had hearing better than my dog's, and had arms long enough to reach past that red M&M and straight into my pounding heart whenever I called for help from under that bed.

"Mom? Dee and I are going to her house, 'kay?" I didn't wait for an answer. I knew by this time she was lost in the land of malt liquor.

There were only two surefire safe places in my world. One of them was Dee Dee's house, and the other—of course—was under my twin bed. I loved going over to Dee Dee's for reasons that are clear to me now. The first thing I loved about it was that they ate dinner every night at 6:00 p.m. sharp. The only confusing part was that often Dee Dee's dad, Sheldon, and Janeen enjoyed T-bone steaks in the dining room while we kids ate weenies 'n beans at the kitchen table. Mom never did that. If she couldn't afford steak for everyone, she didn't buy it for anyone. And we all ate around the same table.

Wolfing down my last bite of hot dog with mustard seeping from the corner of my mouth, Janeen brushed my stringy hair away from my face. "Slow down, Michele, there's plenty, Honey." She didn't know that at our house if you hesitated, you might not get seconds. It was impossible for me to turn that message off just because I was at Dee Dee's house.

The second part I loved about being there was our after-dinner trips to Balboa Island for dessert. We all piled into the Bass family Cadillac and headed for the beach. That was really cool. The salty night air made my hair feel like cotton candy, but it was worth it.

One by one, Dee Dee's dad told the man through the hole in the window at the Banana Shack what flavors we wanted. Dee Dee and I, along with her sisters, Dana and Kimmy, pressed our little noses against the cold, damp glass and watched the guy dip each frozen banana in the liquid chocolate and then quick-roll it in a topping before it turned to a hard shell. I always chose nuts, 'cause I liked the salt mixed with the sweet taste. When the man lifted my banana from the pile of nuts, I prayed none would fall off. Dee Dee always chose rainbow sprinkles so her banana was prettier than mine, but mine tasted better. We laughed and sang all the way home, high on sugar and the feeling of sand tickling us between our toes.

Finally, I loved Dee Dee's house for bathtime.

Dee Dee and I shared a tub of our very own bathwater! We jumped into a bubble-topped tub of fresh, hot water and had endless water fights armed with old baby dolls. We pulled their heads off, filled them full, and shot water out of their eyes and bottoms. I was a better aim than Dee Dee, but sometimes I let her win.

After a quick towel fight, we slipped into clean PJs, and when 8:30 rolled around, Janeen said the words I'd longed to hear all day, "It's bedtime, girls."

"Ah, nuts!" Dee Dee complained. But not me.

I smiled, from ear to ear. Janeen looked past every one of my crooked teeth and straight into my heart. She knew exactly why I was so happy to hit the hay: Dee Dee had a top sheet.

It was tucked so snugly around the mattress you had to pull with all your might to loosen it enough to get in. It was so nice and tight and safe, like being wrapped in a cocoon. Even though the Basses had a Kenmore dryer, Janeen hung the sheets outside to dry in the afternoon breeze. I thought surely God sent angels to breathe on them when nobody was looking.

They were white as snow, soft as marshmallows, and smelled like jellybeans.

I didn't have a top sheet on my twin bed. I barely had a bottom sheet. Sometimes I still wet the bed and didn't always tell Mom about it. The stinky sheets would need to go downstairs the next morning, and I'd need to throw them in the washer before school. If I forgot, I'd have to sleep on a bare bed the next night.

The little buttons on the mattress scratched my legs, and the center was wet with pee. I'd go to the linen closet and fish out a clean beach towel, fold it in two, and press it into the wet spot. I tried not to toss and turn too much during the night. If I did, the feeling of yesterday's cold pee woke me right up. Half asleep, I reached to find the towel and put it back where it belonged.

That's how I knew God didn't live on the topside of my bed. I never would have asked Him to find me there. But when I was in Dee's bed, under her top sheet, I could feel Him all around me. I tried not to close my eyes, but it was a losing battle. The cool, clean, comfy spots made my eyelids heavy every single time.

In mid-1986, after Jesus and I untangled threads enough for me to leave my mom's house for good, I moved to North Hollywood to pursue becoming a commercial actor. The first thing I bought was a new mattress and a decent set of sheets. I washed them faithfully once a week. Still do. And I'm not embarrassed to say that I iron my top sheet with "foofy" spray that smells like lavender. Always have, always will. It helps to chase away smells from the past that still live in my nose. But no store-bought sachet in the whole world smells like the angel's breath on Dee Dee's sheets. My top sheet is a constant reminder that God is with me. He covers me. He makes me to lie down in fresh green cotton.

Days come and go. Most are good, and some are not, but every night is the same to me when I crawl into bed. All's well with the world, especially with me, because God meets me there. Peace overtakes me. It calms my nerves and stills my anxious heart. I take a minute and give thanks for the food in my belly and the roof over my head. When I'm finally still and listening, God's voice whispers sweet things to me, and I find answers to questions I've posed throughout the day. I thank Him that I no longer have to crawl under a bed to find Him, because He's tucked between the sheets of my heart.

I would imagine the very last thing I'll do here on Earth is crawl under my top sheet. The angels will abandon their posts in Dee Dee's backyard and come with godspeed to carry me home. I won't be hard to find. They'll but follow their noses to the fragrance of marshmallows and sweet jellybeans. I'll be where I've always been when this world wears me out.

Until that day, I'll cope and laugh. I'll struggle and press on. I'll celebrate life some days and let go of dreams on others. I'll love the people I love and will ask for grace to love the ones I don't. And each time the sun goes 'round the earth, I'll find solace in the most unlikely of all places: under a clean, pressed, and sweet-smelling top sheet.

Chapter 3

THE POWER OF FORGIVENESS
untangling the knot around my family tree

———

Year: 1990 / **Age:** 35
Place: Long Beach Community Hospital, California

"Breathe, Mama. Breathe!" I wasn't yelling at her but close to it. I steadied my hand and tried again. I was holding the mask that was supplying oxygen to keep her alive, but when she opened her eyes, for whatever reason, she pushed it away.

Mama stared back at me with a look I'd never seen before. It was sheer terror. Her expression said exactly what she was thinking: "I don't want to die!"

I don't want you to die either, Mama. It's all my fault, I thought.

My mother was slipping toward death's doorstep and knew it. Without uttering a word she was screaming, "Wait a minute! I want to go back! I need a do-over. I don't know what I need, but this doesn't feel right! Someone help me. I'm not ready to go!" It was a level of panic that only strikes the human heart when eternal separation from God is palpable and within eyesight. And it was happening to my mother.

All I could do was hold the little plastic tube up to her nose one more time and beg her, plead with her to fight harder. She pushed me away again and said, "Honey! Quick! Go grab my panty hose. They're hanging on the shower door. We've *got* to get outta here!" She gripped the bed rail and tried to sit up and almost pulled the mainline IV out of her jugular vein. I lowered her back down with my forearm.

"God help us," I prayed. "No, Mama. Just lay back down and rest."

When they've pumped you full of a million drugs, and you're not getting enough oxygen to the brain, things begin to unravel. I mean, she was only sixty-eight years old, and I wasn't ready to let her go. She was the only mother I had. She was a father too. Dad left us early on, leaving a hole as big as the Grand Canyon in all four of us girls. Mom did all she could to fill us back up, but there was a hole in the bucket. A bunch of them. Holes punched from generations of addiction, anger, and godless living. At least Mom stayed around. Had she abandoned us, too, my three sisters and I would have been all but orphaned. That's why I loved her so, because she stayed. I stood in the greeting card aisle every year, just before Mother's Day, trying to find that perfect one for her, but Hallmark never came close. I finally gave up and started buying her Father's Day cards as well.

Now, leaning over her bed, I was face-to-face with the day I'd feared and dreaded for as long as I could remember. I think most kids do that. The mere thought of the death of our mothers strikes fear in our young hearts. I often awoke from a dead sleep bawling like a baby, got up and stumbled through the dark, sucking my thumb like a Geiger counter to find wherever it was that she passed out the night before. I'd snuggle in with her and

tuck my bottom against her big belly like a spoon, fo..., ...
knife.

"I love you so much, Mommy," I'd whisper.

"Did you have a nightmare, Honey?" she'd ask.

"Yes, Mama. A real bad one."

"Everything's all right now. I'm here, Booby." And my tears
would start all over again.

"I love you, Mama. I love you, Mama," I'd chant over and
over.

"I love you too, Honey." She'd stroke my hair to help me
sleep.

I thought, *You're here now, but one day you will die.* She tried
to soothe me back to sleep, but my fear interrupted the comfort
she was offering.

Now, years later, my mother was fighting for her life in a
hospital bed she'd probably stood over a thousand times before
in order to put food on our table and clothes on our backs. Mom
had walked these halls for thirty years as a licensed vocational
nurse. She had varicose veins the size of No. 2 pencils up and
down her legs to prove it. She couldn't die now, she just couldn't.

Why?

'Cause, I'd blown it! I'd really blown it.

For weeks before Mom's surgery, I looked and prayed and
waited for just the right moment to nail her down about her
relationship with God—or the lack thereof. But I waited too
long. D-day, the day before her surgery, sneaked up on me. My
blood pressure was kicking my melon with a migraine. I was
chewing aspirin like popcorn, and my head still hurt.

All four of us girls faithfully gathered at Mom's house to serve
up what we hoped wasn't her last meal. When I walked through
the door carrying a homemade banana cream pie, my eldest sister

Margretta took my head off. "What are you trying to do, kill her? There's a million calories in that thing!"

I pinched Margretta's sleeve and pulled her out to the front porch. "Please, Margretta. Let's just try to get along, 'kay? Mom's gonna lose a ton of weight in the days ahead, if she makes it at all."

But there was no consoling Margretta. Her fear was like a lit match in a room of methane gas. She picked a fight with each of us, one by one, until our gathering looked like a crematory. After dinner, Mom was so upset she took less than one nibble of my pie. I felt bound and gagged and couldn't have formulated a three-word sentence about God's love for her by evening's end.

When they wheeled Mom into surgery the next morning with that little blue cap on her head, she looked so frightened. And why not? Her salvation was left hanging in the balance, thanks to me. And now she was post-op, dying, and I was in a panic.

A month earlier, the doctor found a huge aneurism in her aorta during a routine checkup. He cut her from stem to stern to fix the darn thing. During the five-hour procedure, the surgeon got a close-up look at her toxic liver and stomach, along with every other organ he pushed aside to get to the artery.

"So she's a drinker, is she?" The doctor questioned me after her surgery.

"Yes, sir."

"Well, she can never have another drink in her life," he said. "A corner of her liver is shot. I'll be having a stiff talking-to with that woman, but first"—his pause depicted his doubt—"she'll have to walk out of the intensive care unit." His eyes reaffirmed his consuming concern about the outcome.

"I'll do my best with her, sir."

There I go again. Trying to do, trying to fix, trying to cover for my mother.

The doctor didn't know that I was covering my own hindend. I was begging God for a second chance to talk to her about something much more important than her liver.

"I am so sorry, God. If You'll let her live, I promise to ask her about You. Just please give me another chance." I asked Him over and over, and again for good measure.

I sat by Mom's bed for the next month staring at her numbers. I was mistaken for hospital staff more than once and had free access to the supply closet. Being the good little servant was my job, as it always had been. I adored my mother, maybe to a fault, and Margretta hated me for it. I had not forgotten Mom's beatings, her verbal abuse, her threats with knives or even her cutting my bangs with pinking shears and a belly full of brandy. But no matter the abuse, I loved my mom more than life.

On day thirty-one, the head nurse of the ICU pulled me aside and shot straight with me. "This always happens with the smokers. We see it all the time. They survive the damn surgery, and then we can't get their lungs to kick back in. Her cause of death will go down on record as 'complications from surgery.' Truth is, she'll die from smoking cigs. If your mom's blood-oxygen levels don't start going up in the next twenty-four hours, she's gonna die. Make her work that machine, once an hour. Make her do it—if you want her to live." If I weren't afraid enough, the toughness of her words shocked me further into the grim reality of Mom's situation.

I ran to the supply closet and tore open the plastic wrap on a brand-new breathing machine. I looked at the cheap little device with the Made in China sticker on the bottom and felt so powerless. I thought, "It's all come down to this? Your life is in the hands of this little doohickey? They'll bill you $150 for it; it's probably only worth a buck-ninety-nine. But ya know what? It holds the keys to heaven, Mom."

I got mad. Real mad. I marched back into Mom's room and shook her awake! "Okay, Mom, here's the deal: If you don't do this [I wagged the gizmo in front of her nose], you're gonna die. Do you wanna die, Mom?"

Half awake, she shook her head no. But she turned over to go back to sleep.

I was fighting for both of us. If Mom were to die today, I'd spend the rest of my life not knowing where she'd spend eternity. I had prayed for her for almost twenty years, since the day I asked Jesus into my own heart, but she wasn't the least bit interested in asking Him to enter hers. She watched me perform at countless concerts, big and small. She admired my work. Yet none of it seemed to penetrate her heart.

Her reasoning was understandable; Mom was a survivor and an angry one at that. I think the notion, the mere thought of forgiving my father for walking out on us, was something she thought impossible. If knowing God meant she'd have to forgive Dad, then she'd rather skip the whole thing. She'd earned the bitter heart in her chest and held it up like a banner wherever she went. There was no room in her heart for God. And besides, who would she be if she weren't angry? Anger was a sure thing. It was fuel that kept her going, kept her strong.

Mom reminded me of the Sick Man at the Pool.[1] When Jesus confronted the man, He asked if he wanted to be made whole. The guy seemed to think about it! You wouldn't expect the man to hesitate after being ill for thirty-eight years. But "sick" was all he knew. His full-time job was lying by the pool with a million excuses for not getting into the healing waters. He was also so caught up in observing the ritual of how to be healed he didn't recognize the Healer incarnate even though He was standing right in front of him. But, in the end, he landed on his feet. Jesus opened his eyes to who He is and he found what he needed—the will to live, the will to believe in something bigger than his aches and pains. He dropped his excuses by the poolside, picked up his bed, and walked away. That's the ending I was hoping for with my mom. But would I get it? It wasn't looking promising.

When my mother wasn't drinking, she was a great mom. To this day, thanks to her, I can create a full nine-course meal with little to nothing in the cupboard. I combine ingredients Wolfgang Puck wouldn't dream of pairing, and they taste yummy. When Mom found herself staring at the bottom of an empty wallet, she threw her shoulders back and threw a party! An artichoke party! With the kitchen table lined with newspaper and five glasses of milk, she'd call us in for dinner and present a mountain of steaming artichokes, as many as we could eat. Add a side of bread 'n butter and Jell-O for dessert and—voila!—dinner was served.

My sisters and I felt so lucky. We got to eat with our hands that night and pile the artichoke leaves a mile high in the middle of the table. Little did we know that Mom's smile, which stretched from ear to ear, was because she'd dodged catastrophe by finding artichokes on sale for five cents apiece at the farmer's market. Other times she had to swallow her pride and ask a neighbor for spare noodles for dinner.

Then there was the time she called us out to the living room saying, "Jump in the car, girls! We gotta go!" Madeline spoke out, "But it's bedtime, Mom. We're in our PJs," as if Mom couldn't see that.

Running right over Madeline's question, Mom ordered,

"Grab the blanket off your bed, Madeline. Everyone get in the car! Hurry up!"

Madeline knew Mom meant business, so she stopped asking questions and got us moving. Before we could say "Rumpelstiltskin," Marilyn, Madeline, and I were in the backseat of our '57 Chevy. Mom took off down the road like she was trying to outrun the devil. We held on tightly to each other, remembering to blink now and then, so our eyes wouldn't pop out of our heads. We wondered if Mom had finally lost her mind. She turned a hard right and nearly took out Farmer Extine's fencerow. We were flying through his orange grove going forty miles per hour. I wanted to stand up and look out the back window to see who was chasing us, but centrifugal force kept me glued to the bench seat.

Orange tree branches slammed against the hood, grille, and windshield. Sheets of orange juice rained down the windows, making it hard for Mom to see. So she flipped on the wipers, and pulp smeared the glass. She slammed the brake pedal to the floorboard, and we skidded to a stop, just short of barreling through a chain-link fence.

Then, quiet and pitch-dark.

Mom shoved the gearshift on the steering column into park and told us to get out of the car.

"Where are we?" Marilyn asked.

"Just do as I say!" Mom insisted. We stepped out of the car, and our little toes sank into the tilled black dirt. We held up our PJ bottoms so they wouldn't drag. Mom reached out her hand and said, "Here, up ya go. Climb up, and lay down on the roof of the car." Using the bumper as a step stool, we did as she instructed without a single word.

When all of us were in place, lying flat on our backs like

three peas in a pod, Mom tossed Madeline's blanket over us and tucked it around our legs and under our bottoms. "There," she said, and she lay down on the hood.

Without warning she yelled, "Look up!"

Boom, ba-boom, boom! The Disneyland fireworks went off— right over our heads! We all started laughing and banging our heels on the roof of the car. The spectacular show was close enough to touch as the bursts of color reflected in our eyes. We had the best seat in the house!

That was my mom.

She had taken the time to figure out where the back lot of Disneyland butted up to farmer Johnny Extine's orchard. Mom didn't have enough money to get us inside the park, but that didn't stop her. We went back to that same spot all summer long and made sure to be in our front row seats by 9:00 p.m. sharp. It was a Ya-Ya Sisterhood moment I'll never forget.

Looking back, I see that poverty didn't affect my mom's priorities. In fact, just the opposite. She made poverty an adventure! These days, I can get so busy that I often allow the passing of time to rob me of so much. My mother's determination and her love for what really mattered inspires me every day of my life. Every time I face a challenge that tells me I don't have what it takes, I remember where I was when I first felt powerful. I was on the roof of a '57 Chevy, looking up.

"Mom, wake up now," I urged. I poked her a couple of times, but she didn't move. I poked her again, and my heart sank. "Mom. Mom! We have to do your breathing exercises now. Come on, Mom. Wake up. Please, wake up." I walked over to the other side of the bed, so I could see her eyes. They were closed, her pallor gray. But she was still breathing.

I exhaled.

Mom turned over in slow motion and asked me for a few more minutes of sleep. "No, Mom! No. You have to wake up." She sat up, and we worked and worked, every hour on the hour, until her blood-oxygen numbers went up.

A couple of weeks later I wheeled my mother out of Long Beach Community Hospital and brought her to our home in LA. My goal was to see her get all-the-way well.

I wasn't gonna miss my chance this time around. Every minute of every day I looked for lucidity in my mother. I looked for the tiniest crack in the door of opportunity. And then it happened. She was sitting at my kitchen table eating lunch, and I told her the truth. I told her how I'd chickened out.

"It scared me, Mom. You scared me."

"I was scared, too, Honey," she said. "When they wheeled me down the hall toward the operating room, I had the most horrible feeling inside, as if I'd forgotten to do something really important, like when you lose your purse or forget to turn off the iron."

I smiled. I know a Spirit-opened door when I see one.

"Mom, if you had died, I would have had to live forever not knowing if you knew God." I let it sink in. "Mom," my voice was even more tender now. I wanted her to hear the love in my heart and feel the Father's love. "Was there ever a time in your life when you asked Jesus to be your Savior?"

I opened my Bible and walked her through John 3:16—"For God so loved the world that he gave his one and only Son, that whoever believes in him shall not perish but have eternal life."

Mom answered. "Well, I walked down to the altar when I was five—but I did it because the pastor said so. Does that count?"

"I'm not sure, Mom. But we both can be sure right now. If

you'll give Him your life, if you'll ask Him for forgiveness, He will come into your heart, Mom. Wanna pray?"

"Sure."

And there it was. The moment I prayed about for twenty years was here. God pulled her through. He'd pulled her through so much, most importantly her unforgiveness. Facing death had rolled the stone of bitterness aside just enough that she could give herself permission to forgive and to be forgiven.

That's what I've discovered. Forgiveness is a weapon of love, if it's nothing else. When I lost everything and was sitting on that twin bed with Jesus, one of the first tangled strings we tackled was my desperate need to forgive my mother and father, but I didn't understand the gravity. I'd spent my whole life tethered to their mistakes. My life carried by-products of their alcohol abuse and all that goes with it. It was all playing itself out in polar opposites in me. I was the pendulum-swing contrast of my parents, becoming in many ways their antithesis. Yet, I was the victim, weak and trying to earn a feeling of importance, of value. I'd spent years trying to compensate for that shame. I picked abusive men. I chose abusive friends. I felt powerless in relationships, especially in my relationship with God. I jumped through hoops for everyone, even God. He didn't ask that of me; I just didn't know what a healthy relationship looked like. I cared too much about what other people wanted and hadn't the foggiest idea of what I needed. Living that way was a form of idolatry. God used Matthew 10:34–36 to open my eyes. In this very unique verse, Jesus said He did not come with peace but with a sword to separate mother from daughter, father from son.

Before I could forgive my mother, the umbilical cord between us had to be severed. God was the only one who could cut it in two. After His sword did the all-important deed, I was free to forgive her, and God gave me the power to do it. After all, He forgave first. He did it perfectly, using every drop of His innocent blood, and set it in stone with the most powerful words ever spoken: "It is finished."[2]

"In Jesus' name, amen" were our last words at the kitchen table during my mother's first prayer. When we opened our eyes, our faces were damp with tears. "Whew," I said to myself, feeling like I'd just crossed the biggest finish line in the world.

After I forgave Mom in 1985, we were never the same again. This paradigm shift meant I no longer needed to please or punish her. Her critical words lost their sting, because I wasn't depending on her approval for my life's blood and oxygen. Our conversations were couched with love, not blame. When God cut that umbilical cord, I was free, free from every hooligan on my family tree. I didn't feel the need to tell Mom I'd forgiven her. That's how I knew it had worked. Forgiveness opened the pathway for the Holy Spirit to move in, soften her heart, and open her eyes. She could finally hear about God with me as the messenger, but only after I'd forgiven her.

Whenever I'm tempted to hold on to unforgiveness, I'm reminded of Mom's fear-stricken eyes in the ICU. But then I flash to the joy of her salvation shining through them after we prayed over a half-eaten turkey sandwich. The power of forgiveness paved the way for her, so that sixty-eight years of pain could be washed away, and the name Florence Lorraine Zarges could be written in the Lamb's book of life.[3]

God gave me a dress rehearsal for letting my mama go, and it was a good thing He did. When she passed away two years later, she did so without warning and all alone. Her heart had given out, or maybe it just floated up to heaven, like a helium balloon—no longer weighted down by the cares of this world. I was out singing in Austin, Texas, the night before she passed. It was never my custom to call her on the phone before an event. But tonight I needed to hear her voice before going down for the sound check. We talked for just a minute, about nothing really. The last thing she said to me was, "I love you, Honey. I'll see you when you get home." Those were the last words I would ever hear from her this side of heaven.

"And you were so right, Mama; I'll see you the minute I get home. I can hardly wait, Mama. I can hardly wait."

Chapter 4

FOUND
untangling the knot of regret

———

Year: 1973 / **Age:** 17
Place: Orange County Medical Center's back bungalows

I had on powder-blue shorts. Any shorter and they'd have qualified as bikini bottoms. I sat there in a little metal chair, bouncing my knees up and down, trying to stay warm. The backs of my legs on the cold metal sent shivers up my spine and made my teeth chatter with every bounce. In reality, it was a big, bad case of nerves.

My cuffed, crisp linen shorts came as part of a suit with a really cute matching jacket, but I left that part at home, not wanting to draw attention to myself.

Too late for that.

I had worn the skimpy number twelve hours earlier when I won the title of Miss Westminster. When they called out my name as the new city queen, I strutted down the runway like a gazelle with a Pepsodent smile! My long, sun-kissed legs pouring out of those little shorts helped seal the deal, but sexy gams can also walk a girl straight into big trouble. And that's what I was in this morning: big trouble. The glory of the night before faded into the dingy, army green walls now surrounding me. I sat flipping through the pages of a beaten-up *Seventeen* magazine. It was stained and dog-eared from countless other girls who'd sat here before me killing time. I sighed and replayed last night's victory, remembering what a nightmare it was.

Winning a beauty pageant is usually a girl's dream-come-true, but I was blinded by the spotlight and deafened from the sound of the roaring crowd. It was all I could do to walk that runway without slipping, tripping, or falling off my stilettos and into the judges' laps. Little did they know, it felt to me more like walking a ship's plank. "Steady on. You can do this, Michele. They'll never have to know your secret," I said to myself, putting one foot in front of the other. What I didn't count on was catching my mother's eye in the audience. The moment our eyes met, I broke into tears for reasons I hoped she would never know. I covered my tracks by placing my hand over my heart, throwing her a kiss, pretending I was overtaken with joy. I deserved more than a crown last night—I deserved an Academy Award.

My skin had a healthy glow, ten watts brighter than all the other contestants in the pageant, a glow that doesn't come from good eating habits or exceptional genes but from the genetics growing alive and well inside of me.

Walking through the doors of this dank place was much harder than I thought it would be. It made last night's runway stroll seem like a cakewalk. Being here at this clinic was as icky as putting on a wet bathing suit.

If the judges knew I was here this morning, they'd never have given me the crown, I thought. Who in their right mind wears the very shorts she wore in a pageant to a place like this? I mean, the same shorts that appeared on the cover of today's newspaper—the *Orange County Register,* for goodness' sake? A pair of jeans or even baggy sweats and large sunglasses would have been a smarter choice, but I didn't know any better—that's how lost I was.

I kept telling myself there was no other way but to come here to this God-forsaken place. My mother would be devastated if she knew I was pregnant. She had disappointments enough to last a lifetime. She didn't need another one.

I would be graduating from high school in a couple of months and would enroll in Golden West College next week. The first-ever Commercial Music Department was kicking off at GWC in the fall, and the staff members were proud of their new curriculum. They'd courted me for months and were thrilled I was coming. I couldn't wait to get there.

Besides all that, how does a girl stand on a moving float and wave to the crowd if she's green with morning sickness? I could just see it now: "Excuse me, Mr. Float Chauffeur. Can we pull over for a second so I can bow at the waist and barf curbside, please?"

And I doubted the Westminster Chamber of Commerce would welcome the idea of gown alterations to accommodate my ever-changing belly. Ribbon-cutting ceremonies could get sticky too. During my last trimester, I'd have a heck of a time reaching over my tummy to maneuver those extra-large pretend scissors. I'd never heard of a beauty queen who looked as if she swallowed a basketball. Besides, the biggest responsibility and honor a queen is asked to perform is representing her fair city in the Miss Orange County Pageant, the largest county in the state of California. Should she win Miss OC, she'd be the top seed for Miss California and hopefully go on to win the coveted Miss America crown. When the judges placed that scepter in my arms last night, they didn't picture a baby beside it. Believing I was the future Miss America, they were already patting themselves on the back for their ability to choose a winner.

These cold, hard facts were obstacles I couldn't see around, sitting in the little metal chair. That's why I came here to the county abortion clinic to make it right, to buy myself more than time, to buy myself the future I wanted. I was kicking myself for being stupid enough to wind up pregnant. Jim, the baby's father, was eight years my senior and taught art classes at the high school down the street from mine. The impropriety of statutory rape didn't cross my mind until years later and was more than I could deal with at the moment anyway.

To top it off, Jim's dad was my high school music teacher. I was the star pupil of his thirty-year career. If Mr. Sutherland found out about this, he would jump for joy, throw us a party and the biggest wedding in history. That thought scared me even more than sitting in this hallway did. Nevertheless, when Jim refused to pay for the abortion, I snapped back at him, saying, "That's okay. I'll just go ask your father for the money. He'd be more than happy to help me!"

Jim whipped out his checkbook so fast it practically blew my false eyelashes off! I was surprised at my courage and proud of myself for coming up with such a strong comeback. I didn't feel strong, though. I was heartbroken. I snatched the check from his grubby hand and barely made it back to my VW Bug before falling apart.

I drove here to the county hospital all by myself. And now I was waiting, uncertain of exactly what for. I'm sure there were other girls sitting in their own little metal chairs beside me, but my memory has erased their faces. I only remember me sitting there.

A side door opened, and a woman came out. She pulled up a metal chair of her own. It scraped across the ancient tile floor with the sound of a screaming child. She plopped herself down right in front of me. She was holding a clipboard, and her face bore a huge smile.

"I have great news for you!" she said.

My heart sprang a leak of hope. It was the first positive thing I'd felt since before discovering I was pregnant. She went on. "A new law has just passed, and it's only ninety days old. It's called Roe v. Wade. Now you have choices."

I looked deep into her eyes, searching for something that made more sense than an abortion. Even though seventeen and scared to death, I didn't want one. In my youthful, selfish state, even I knew the difference between right and wrong, and this all felt very wrong to me. But what were my choices? What magical solution did this woman have up her sleeve or on the front side of that clipboard? I listened with both ears.

"Although a minor, you don't have to tell your parents about having this procedure," she began. (I pictured my mother's face. My dad's never came to mind.) Okay. Now I was confused.

That's not a choice, lady. That's more like a right, I thought but didn't say. I listened on, wishing I had another ear.

"You don't have to tell the father of the baby," she said.

Oops. Already did. He ran like the wind, lady. But again, I didn't say a word.

My hopes began to wane.

"This procedure is simple and safe. You'll come out of it just fine, thanks to our new technology." The lady said these things with beaming pride and then went into great detail about the new machine. I stopped listening altogether at this point. It was more than I cared to know.

Okay, lady. You're telling me everything I need to know about having a secret abortion, but what about options, choices? Questions were screaming in my head, but like a lamb to the slaughter, I made no protest.

Even though in a fog of confusion, I was tracking better than this lady was. She started her spiel with the word *choices* and then didn't give me even one. When Dee Dee, Dana, Kimmy, and I pressed our noses against the glass at the Banana Shack, the guy wearing the wedge cap pointed out our choices one at a time. He looked closely and watched us as he waved the banana over the toppings until our eyes told him what we wanted. Would it be sprinkles, coconut, nuts, or maybe no topping at all? (That was always Kimmy's choice.) Maybe even no banana at all! Maybe we wanted cotton candy or popcorn.

As I looked at the lady in the metal chair, I couldn't help but wish the man from the Banana Shack was the one holding the clipboard. Now those were choices! But that seemed light years ago; this was a whole other lifetime, colder and harder than the metal chairs that supported this hopeless conversation.

By this time my head was swimming. I liked the idea of point #1: not telling my mom. Point #2 was moot in my case. And so was point #3, because the word *procedure* made it sound like I was there to get my teeth cleaned or get a fresh haircut. But I knew better. I somehow also knew I wouldn't come out of this thing "just fine," as the counselor promised.

I wondered who had stolen this lady's heart and buried it somewhere far away from her chest? And her soul? Where did it go? How could she make a living doing this with such calm resolve? And how could she muster that smile? Maybe she found mine, the one I lost last night at the beauty pageant. These questions, and many more, were the ones I wondered about but couldn't formulate into coherent thoughts.

I wish I could go back in time to 1973, pull out a clipboard, and ask that counselor some questions of my own: "Okay, lady, tell me when it was you talked yourself into this? How do you sleep at night? Or does the sound of that new, fancy machine keep you up at night, like it does me, so many years later?" I'd love to hear her explain it to both of us—me and the seventeen-year-old me.

One week later, wearing my now-wrinkled powder-blue shorts for the third time, I drove back to that back-lot bungalow and had an abortion.

I fulfilled my duties as Miss Westminster like a good girl should. I cut ribbons all year and waved from moving floats without a single spill or tossing my cookies. Somewhere along the way I found the semblance of a smile, but my skin lost its glow altogether.

I didn't go on to the Miss California Pageant; instead of me, a sweet, little blonde girl named Michelle Pfeiffer, representing the neighboring city, Fountain Valley, won the title of Miss Orange County. I came away with third place, or as they call it in pageant lingo, I "won second runner-up."

Michelle Pfeiffer didn't go on to the Miss California Pageant either, though. She quit the circuit to follow her dreams as an actress. I think she made a wise choice. I missed taking her place by one notch because of my third-place ranking. Yes, I sang like a bird in college and realized my dreams as a recording artist but all under the cloud of my abortion. I did my best to put the past behind me, but I never really succeeded at it.

The lady with the clipboard sitting in the metal chair was

wrong on every count. She didn't know what she didn't know, and she couldn't see the future.

Jim, my baby's father, was in an accident two years later that rendered him a paraplegic. He'd never have another child.

My mother pulled me aside years later and told me that if abortion had been available to her in 1955 when she became pregnant with me, I wouldn't be alive today. She went on to say, "With three daughters by my side and your father all but gone, the last thing I needed was another mouth to feed." With tears streaming down her face, she continued her confession. "Losing you would have been the single biggest mistake of my life."

That's when I told my mom about my abortion in 1973 and why I didn't tell her about it sooner. We sat on my couch in Los Angeles, held hands, and cried for all we'd lost so long ago.

I didn't need the man from the Banana Shack or the lady with the clipboard for guidance in 1973. I needed my mother. I was a child "with child." I needed her ears, her questions, her perspective, and her support. And my mother didn't need my protection. I know that now.

That was the day I faced the chilling realization that if Roe v. Wade had passed in the 1950s, I—along with more than a third of the seventy-nine million baby boomers—never would have been born. The likes of Steve Jobs, James Taylor, and Tom Hanks—gone.

This world would be a different place without any one of us who exists. I never would have lived to love, to sing, and to tell my mom about Jesus. She and I never would have been a "we" at all, and I wouldn't be typing these words.

And as far as point #3 goes, I didn't come out of it "just fine," as I knew I wouldn't. My left leg ached for six months after my abortion, and the doctors didn't know why. I never became pregnant again, even when I tried to. Was I broken? Had they broken me? Was it a physical brokenness? Maybe it was the deep sense of guilt and shame that kept my body from giving me another child. Not one doctor could answer those questions. By the time God stepped in and answered them for me, I was in my forties and too old to bear children.

These are only a few of the things the lady in the metal chair couldn't see. She couldn't see around corners, she couldn't see Jim's future, and she didn't know my mother's past. And she couldn't see how I was wired—to punish myself for the next thirty years. So, this pregnancy would be my last pregnancy, my only pregnancy. That lady wasn't God, and neither was I; yet we both acted as if we were.

I asked Jesus to be my Savior three weeks after my abortion. My trip to the county hospital broke me from the inside out, and God was right there to pick up the pieces. He now had my undivided attention, and He didn't use my abortion against me. I needed help from someone who could see around corners. I could see that, now. Before my abortion, I never felt like I'd done anything wrong enough to merit someone dying in my place. I was a good kid. Got good grades. Didn't do drugs or drink. But after my abortion, my eyes were pried open. I knew that if an eye for an eye[1] was God's law, then I owed Him my life for the one I'd taken. But the beauty was, He would only ask me to give Him my life for the sake of following Him, knowing Him, and allowing Him to love me and live in me for the rest of my life.

Coming to know Jesus was bittersweet, because I was still recovering from my abortion. My heart felt a deeper love than I'd ever known, but my body was torn to shreds. I was in so much pain. During one of my many post-op doctor visits, a nurse said,

"They must have hit a nerve up there." (She said it like it was nothing.) *They hit a nerve, all right,* I thought. *One that starts in my heart and goes all the way to China.*

I was so thankful finally to know the name of the Person who'd been there to protect me as a young child. His name was Jesus, yet I couldn't help but wish I'd met Him three weeks earlier. I moved on with my life with Jesus in my heart but was unable to embrace total forgiveness about my abortion. Since I couldn't see how broken I was, asking God for help wasn't on my radar. For years I lived believing Jesus died for everything except my abortion.

This subtle torment caught me off guard when I least expected it. The moment I stepped onto platforms like the Billy Graham Crusades, shame covered me like a blanket. It felt like the recurring dream I had as a child, where I was walking to grammar school on a windy day in a crinoline skirt and realized I wasn't wearing underwear. I hated that dream! That's how I felt at the Graham Crusades and countless other public appearances after my abortion: uncovered and ashamed.

This secret shame was a foe that wouldn't let me be. He was the uninvited guest who acted inappropriately at formal occasions, like a Lampshade Louis following me around through life. He was distracting. He weakened me when I needed to feel strong and good about myself. *What's he doing here?* became my focus instead of *What am I doing here?* This foe made it hard for me to enjoy life and my accomplishments and blinded me from seeing that I was blessed. I felt helpless and like an impostor. I didn't know how to ask for help, because I was too ashamed to talk about it with anyone, especially God.

I stopped singing and touring in the mid-1990s for many reasons, not the least of which was the shame. Untangling. Untangling. Untangling the shame. It took time and lots of it. It took shining a light on it and dousing it in God's opinion of me in light of His promises. Now, out of the limelight, I was in no hurry. I just wanted to be free from the heebie-jeebies.

I wanted peace. I wanted someone to lower the tightrope so I could step down. I disappointed so many people when I stopped working. Cash flow stopped. People lost their jobs and, for a people-pleaser like me, it felt like professional suicide. In many ways it was. But as each knot broke loose, I knew I'd done the right thing when I stepped away from ministry. In my mind my singing career was over for good.

But this new spiritual boot camp landed me somewhere between solitary confinement and heaven on Earth—a double-edged sword to say the least, and the honeymoon wore thin. I didn't know who I was without my music, and God wanted to change that. But the roots ran deep. I'd buried all my skeletons under my music. The more dirt I piled on top of old wounds, the more they began to stink. That burial ground ushered spiritual and emotional death into my life.

I was bound to my shame and to the shame of others that had been slapped upon my life. God would need to change that, too. It was a push-and-pull process. I doubted myself, and I doubted God at every turn. I kicked and screamed. I protested and felt sorry for myself. I hated feeling like a nobody. The process was taking too long.

Voices in my head told me I was unfixable: born this way or that; I was being punished and would never be whole, never worthy to sing about God again. I wished I could go back and change my mind about untangling these knots, these mind-sets. I wanted God to stop, but I would have had to leave Him behind to make that happen. I couldn't. I knew better now, so I kept walking, listening, learning. God was uncoiling a thick metal spring inside me. When the tension finally snapped loose, I loved who I was without my music. I loved the peace of mind. I loved belonging to Him and Him only. I loved trashing the hamster wheel. I loved laughing despite my past and letting go of the house I grew up in. I was a hostage to neither one any longer.

Years passed, and low 'n behold, in 2005 I was walking through my barn, minding my own business, when God spoke to my heart, *It's time to lighten your load. It's time to go back into ministry.* I shook it off. I tried to ignore it. I'd gotten really good at being alone. I was happy with "alone." I was succeeding at this thing called life and didn't want to rock the boat. Honestly, I was afraid to return to the scene of the crime.

My job now was working and managing a small horse-breeding program with a staff of three: me, myself, and I. It was a far cry from teetering crowns and Grammy telecasts, but it felt good, really good. Every day began the same way, feeding horses and mucking stalls. I stacked hay in August and worked with the mares and their babies in the snow and ice. I took on the roles of midwife and vet and slept in the barn with one eye open, listening for water bags to break. I marketed and sold the foals and made just enough profit each year to keep it all going.

Now and then I sang at church, and I served on the executive board of the not-for-profit organization Closer to Home to assist the needy in my community. That was all the ministry I needed. Life was calm, cool, and collected.

But I couldn't deny this stirring to reenter the ministry. *Maybe it's a midlife crisis,* I told myself. But it was constant and unrelenting. *God's gifts are without reproach* went through my head more than once. I asked God for further instruction, as if I didn't understand, but He was silent. I'd hear nothing more from Him until I'd done what He'd already asked of me to lighten my load.

I gave in, and I found new owners for my mares, Nandie and Breeze, as well as their offspring. I cried when the last horse left the farm, but that was replaced with the urge to write. Exhuming my atrophied gifts felt like pulling an old car out of the garage, dusting it off from hood ornament to tail pipe to figure out what still worked and what needed to be replaced. When I got confused or discouraged, God would simply say, *Tell the truth, Michele. Tell the truth.* For the next two years His prodding was always the same.

So I did. I told the truth. I wrote about everything the best way I knew how. I shed light on what happens to a Christian who falls down as hard as I did, in hopes it would make its way to someone out there who needed to know.

Then, one day it hit me: The shame was gone, and so was the pain. It was as if I was writing about someone else's life. My secrets were like a basket of old laundry. I could hold them up for display and point out the moth holes, stains, rips, and tears, because the garments no longer fit me, were out of style, and I'd never dream of putting them on again. I love that about God. Walking with Him in truth changes everything, and it happens in the calm, quiet places almost without our knowing it. While I'd been going about my mundane life, God was busy working to untangle thread after thread.

Writing, creating again, felt like waking up from a very long nap. I called my friends BeBe Winans and Chris Eaton and asked if they'd like to get together and write a song. Both said yes, and we found a day that worked for us.

The night before our writing date, I crawled into bed and asked God what He wanted us to write about. "I don't have anyone to answer to but You."

I don't remember closing my eyes. I don't remember falling asleep. I didn't fall down a deep hole like Alice in Wonderland did, but I found myself walking through a wonderland just the same. I was floating over a brilliant, stunning green meadow that would make the greens of this world appear gray.

There was a low-lying mist kissing the top of the grass, and a tiny cabin was nestled in the tree line. Smoke rose from the chimney of the sweet cottage, and animals of every variety inhabited the meadows, grazing, sleeping, and wandering around.

I was walking toward the cabin when the door burst open, and out ran hundreds and hundreds of little children of varying ages. They were coming out to play, and the sound of their voices was the most beautiful thing I'd ever heard. They were singing, dancing, laughing, jumping rope, and clapping their hands. None of them could see me, so I stopped, stood still, and drank it all in.

Then, one child's eyes caught mine.

He looked about ten months old, and he waddled his way through the crowd, making his way to me. I pushed through as well, trying to get to him as quickly as I could. Closer and closer we made our ways. When we were within an arm's length, he reached for me and I for him, and he grabbed my little finger. The minute we touched, I knew who he was.

He was mine.

Every fiber of my being focused on my son. Every cell in me underwent a momentary job change: to memorize every detail my senses could gather about him. I could hear my son's heart beating strong and true, and long-awaited relief filled my soul. He looked into my eyes with nothing but love, and without saying a word said, "It's okay."

Before I could respond, he smiled, turned, and walked away. I tried to follow him, but he melted into the sea of children, off to play, off to dance, off to live. He sang a song, and the others sang along, "It's okay, my mother's here. It's okay for God is near. It's okay, for I am found . . . in the Land of Forever where life abounds."

I awoke with a start, crying like a baby.

Once again, a knot, the deepest one to date, was loosened and freed—a knot lost so deep in memory that God had to anesthetize me to reveal it.

God wants me to write a song about my abortion, I thought. I cracked a smile—a real one, the one I lost the night of the pageant in 1973.

As I got ready to leave to write with BeBe and Chris, I replayed the dream over and over in my head. I burned into my heart the image of my son's face, along with his hands, feet, toes, and hair. And his smile—I'll never forget his smile.

Most of all I remembered "It's okay."

What I really wanted to do was to skip the writing session altogether and run back to bed to find my son again, living in the Land of Forever, but I knew I couldn't. The dream had done its job. It began the process of a healing long overdue and birthed the new song "Found."

But before "Found" would be written, there was one more thing to be done.

My courage flew out the car window on the drive to the writing session. I wondered, *What will people think? Will they question my sanity? Maybe things like this are better left unsaid, left in secret, Michele.*

God said nothing.

I recalled sitting in the rickety metal chair in that dingy, green hallway at the abortion clinic wearing my powder-blue shorts. Only this time I had duct tape over my mouth and around my feet and hands, unable to speak, unable to move, unable to get up and walk out of there. I was unable to defend myself from the pillage that was about to rob me of motherhood and take my son's life. But this time I did something about it. "No more!" I shouted, driving on I-65. "No more! Not this time around!" I think every driver on the road could hear me. "*No more!* Not again, Michele! Not this time, lady with the clipboard!" I shouted, and my courage returned on the wings of my words.

God's voice chimed in, loud and clear. *It's time to heal, Michele. But first, it all has to come into the light! Tell the truth. It's time to tell Me everything, Michele, and then tell the world.*

My tears fell like rain as this epiphany filled my heart and mind. *You, Lord, are the Truth, and I never again want to be afraid to tell You everything. You trump all my truths, my secrets, my shame, my knots!* I exhaled.

Tell the truth, tell the truth, rang in my ears. I understood for the first time that telling the truth means telling God everything.

I nearly pulled the car over to the side of the road. I was crying so hard I soaked the back of my sleeve, wiping my eyes to see the road. I kept driving as I cried out to God.

I told the Lord everything I could remember about my abortion. I allowed myself to recall all I had imagined about what happened to my baby that day. Everything my body felt inside my innocent womb. Every sound, every jab . . . everything. Every detail I tried so hard to bury in 1973 came flooding back. I confessed my false belief that abortion is unforgivable and mourned the lie that I wasn't worthy to have other children. I told God how sad that felt to me, now that I knew better. I screamed out to the father of lies and laughed in his face, telling him he didn't win after all! I told God how sorry I was. I thanked Him for taking me to where my son lives now and forever. I thanked God that my son didn't really die in 1973, that he was alive and whole from the instant he left my body. With each word of our conversation, I felt my long-awaited healing taking place.

Knot after knot after ancient knot. *Gone, gone, gone.*

I'd always believed that horrible imaginings, etched in the mind like Polaroid pictures, can't be erased—only lived with. I know better now. The truth can change those images. My son is alive. He is beautiful. Whole. All the lost children are. Since my dream, I'll never see them any other way.

I walked though Chris Eaton's front door without a speck of mascara on my eyelashes and gazed at BeBe through swollen eyelids. I told them about my dream, and they listened with tender hearts. I finished by saying, "But I don't know how to do this. How do we say so much in a three-minute song?" As long as I live I'll never forget BeBe's response: "You had a dream, 'Chele. We have to try."

And try we did. Chris sat at the keyboard and played the kind of chords that only Chris Eaton can play. BeBe and I sat together holding up the living room wall and, with pen and paper in hand, BeBe spoke the words, "They were lost, now they're found" for the very first time. We watched as this beautiful portrait of a song was birthed in honor of the unborn. We worked for hours until the last note of "Found" was on paper.

Today, as I write, is Easter Sunday morning 2010. New life is in the air. The words "It is finished!" dance though my head and circle 'round my heart. Where would I be without the promise of new life? Where would my son be? Things done in the dark and sealed in the grave of time and choice are no match for the resurrected Christ! He breathed life into the lungs of a helpless, voiceless baby boy in 1973 and offered forgiveness to his mother decades later in 2006. But it came only after she opened her heart, opened her mouth, and asked for the Truth to reveal the truth to her and set her free.

"To dream the impossible dream. To fight the unbeatable foe," a songwriter once penned. I think he was wrong. There is no foe unbeatable. Who is this foe the writer speaks of? Is it the woman holding the clipboard? Is it the doctor who went to work that morning and took my child's life? Is it me?

No.

The foe is silence. So, I speak. To individuals, to groups, to a broken world, and I tell the truth, everything, especially that Jesus' obedient, sacrificial act is greater than any act or deed I have ever done, greater than what any of us has ever done.

And because I speak, this foe has no choice but to run and hide—back to the darkness, back to the deafening silence, to a place where there are no children playing, no babies singing, no mothers healing, and no life everlasting. This foe has no place where everything lost is finally found.

Chapter 5

EATING CROW AND KEEPING IT DOWN
untangling the impossible task—paying penance

Year: 1989 / **Age:** 34
Place: our house in Sand Canyon, California

*C*all me crazy, but the Beatles, chocolate, and God have always been synonymous in my world. These three sources of strength, passion, and joy found me, not the other way around. One by one, each revealed its purpose and meaning in my life, but only one of them had a plan, a way of escape, a route to relief, a plan when there seemed to be no plan in sight. And for that I am grateful.

As far as the Beatles are concerned, that's easy. They mowed me over, plain and simple. I loved them from the moment I heard their first note. From the first beat, they made me feel alive. They made me want to dance and be free. They taught me how to sing harmony when I could barely tie my own shoes and later made my heart pound for true love. They made me believe that all things wonderful were waiting for me just outside my bedroom walls.

Chocolate is a longer, different story altogether, because I
didn't start off with a hankering for the stuff like most girls do.
I know that's weird and very lack-o-progesterone of me. I've
often wondered if there was something seriously wrong with me.
Like, maybe I possess a nano-speck of a Y chromosome, which
cancels out the womanly desire for this creamy confection. I've
even gone as far as pretending I like chocolate more than I do
when I'm at baby showers and slumber parties, just to fit in.
Most women use chocolate as a drug, but not me. Salt is my fix.
Give me a big bag of chips and a bowl of hot salsa, and I'm in
heaven. And blue cheese?! There's nothing better in the whole,
wide world. When my heart gives out one day, it—more than
likely—will be from too much blue cheese, not from one of
those "Death by Chocolate" desserts. For years I accepted these
personal quirks, until one day when one, single bite of chocolate changed absolutely everything in my world . . . forever.

"God? I can't do this. I'm just not good at it. And besides,
I'm having a very hard time. Well, I'm having an extremely difficult time accepting the fact that one mistake, amortized over
thirty years, equals a life of misery. I'm telling You, I can't deal
with that!" I complained.

I walked through the halls of our house in LA mumbling to
God under my breath as I, for the umpteenth time, went around
flushing unflushed toilets, picking up wet, stinky towels from
my stepchildren's bedroom and bathroom floors and one excep-
tionally wet towel draped over my side of our bed.

Do they do this at their mother's house? I wondered. *Do they
come by it honestly? Maybe she encourages water conservation,
and that's why they never flush, even after going #2. Yeah, right,
Michele, keep on kidding yourself. If that were the case, they'd
remember to turn off the lights and wouldn't leave the faucets*

dripping incessantly. Remember the other day wh
left the refrigerator door wide open and the mi
it, girl, they hate you. Their mother hates you. And deep ...
heart, I couldn't blame them.

That's how it was every other weekend when my husband's
two children, Katie and Travis, came to stay with us. I cooked, I
cleaned. They played, they complained. About anything, about
everything that wasn't like their mother's way of doing things.

We'd sit down to eat dinner, and it would start. "I like Mom's
fried chicken better," Travis announced and poked around at his
food like it was contaminated. Then tension fell like a smart
bomb, and the air was so thick you could cut it with a knife,
until we were done eating.

Mom doesn't make us do the dishes. Katie sent me the message via mental telepathy and bolted from the table to play more
Nintendo.

I was left looking at the aftermath of my efforts in futility.
Every dirty dish, pot, pan, dinner plate, fork, knife, and yuck stared
back at me as if to say, "You made your bed, girl. Now lie in it!"

Our kitchen was the perfect picture of our life: it was a mess.
With fried chicken and mashed potatoes barely down my gul-
let, my first order of business was to crawl under the table on
my hands and knees to pick up the tiny pieces of corn, bread
crumbs, and chicken cracklings that our table was somehow
insufficiently large enough to catch. Then it was on to clearing
the table, washing the dishes, and finally sweeping the floor,
trying to rid myself of flour, salt, pain, and humiliation. And
where was my husband? I can't remember. But he wasn't helping me with the mess. He was probably upstairs dealing with
our mess of a family by playing video games with the kids, trying to make it all up to them.

When a family gets split down the middle and becomes two families, it's a mess. For a long time it's a mess. I read three step-parenting books before Larry and I wed. To help make the transition easier for the kids, three years passed before we married. Once we took that step, I never in a million years would have asked to have a child of my own. It only would have made things worse. If the subject arose, Larry's usual response was, "I didn't do a good job with the kids I have. I shouldn't have any more."

Subject closed.

And while we're on the subject of kids, the two in our house were the ones holding the reins in this new arrangement. We adults were just treading water, trying to keep our noses above the waves of guilt. We were good at smiling, good at buying, and great at small talk. Yet right behind our pearly whites brewed rage, anger, blame, and sorrow.

Blended families are difficult at their best and catastrophes at their worst. Ours was definitely the latter. But what did I expect? Our beginnings were upside down and backward. Our roots were riddled with grubs and cutworms. You can't ever change your false start. Beginnings, good or bad, are carved in the bedrock of time.

The holidays were the worst. "What shall we give Cyndie for Christmas, Honey?" I asked Larry. He looked at me like a deer in headlights and answered. "I don't know, Michele. Look for something nice." As if I should know what to buy his former wife, for heaven's sake!

"I don't know" was his answer to almost every question I posed about our new family. "If I had a nickel for every time you've said 'I don't know' to me, Larry, I'd be a millionaire." I glared back at him.

When Larry would say "I don't know," I would hear "I don't care." What he really was trying to say to me was "I don't understand how to make this right, how to make this better. I'm stumped."

Helpless is what we were. Stuck in the past. Stuck in the rut of the damage. Stuck. Stuck. Stuck.

I walked through the mall every December trying to figure out what gift to buy Cyndie for Christmas. What was too much? What was not enough? What message would the gift send? It makes me tired thinking about it now. Maybe no gift at all would have been a good practice to start with, but gifts were my way of making it all up to her. It was my way of pretending we were a happy, healthy family. My way of saying I was sorry. And besides, I liked Cyndie, yet that never seemed to be something I could convey to her. And that's understandable. Why would she think I liked her? I hurt her. I'm sure that's what she felt when she looked at me. Men and women usually choose the same sort of people for partners again and again. When I looked at Cyndie, I saw myself. The fact that their marriage failed despite their efforts instilled in me an empathy for her.

Our family's pain was as big as an elephant dancing in the living room, and you'd think pain that big would be impossible to ignore. Yet, if we were good at only one thing, we were experts at ignoring the dancing beast. He wore a saddle called guilt; a bridle called the past; and wore four very pointed toe shoes called shame, blame, denial, and unforgiveness. We called ourselves followers of Christ, yet the elephant was calling the shots and stepping all over our toes, souls, hearts, and minds. His goal was to make certain we'd never have a future absent the pain of the past.

How did I get here? I wondered many times. *Everything was going along just fine before I met Larry, or was it?* I asked myself.

I had been married to a pretty good guy, and we had a good life. But the elephant was dancing in our living room too. We, like

Cyndie and Larry, were ignoring him at every turn. My previous husband Steve and I were so busy riding the wave of my success, we couldn't hang on to much else. I was on the road two hundred days a year telling the world about Jesus, yet Jesus was not allowed in the inner sanctums of our marriage. *Heaven forbid, we should have flaws!* was our mind-set.

I didn't want to disappoint everyone who was counting on me to be strong, to be an example, and to sell lots of records. I started off strong ten years before and didn't realize I'd lost my legs until they were already gone. Steve and I had stopped going to church. We told ourselves that we were too tired and deserved to sleep in on Sunday mornings, but in hindsight I see that we needed to be in church more than we needed shut-eye.

Just like in 1973, when I was sitting in the cold metal chair at the county clinic, I didn't speak up. Not enough, anyway. I asked for time off but didn't put my foot down hard enough. I didn't express my need for help in a way anyone could hear the depth of my need. Instead, I acted out my frustrations. What I was about to do to be heard seemed like an act of bravery at the time, but now I see it as cowardice, controlling, self-centered, and plain old foolishness. Age-old sin was all it was, the kind that drove Jesus Christ up a hill called Golgotha to spill His blood for people just like me.

"Watch this!" I said to the whole world. And in one fell swoop I pulled the plug on everything by having an affair with Cyndie's husband, Larry. In not wanting to disappoint anyone, I disappointed everyone—most of all, God. And myself. I shocked the world as I shocked myself and took what wasn't mine.

Larry and I met at the Grammy Awards in 1984. I was nominated for two awards that February evening and was a presenter on the telecast. Larry was nominated for the film score *Against*

All Odds. He was a young Christian and wanted to be a part of the Christian music industry. I was getting ready for my third recording for Sparrow Records and was looking for a new producer. From the minute we met, sparks flew. I've asked myself *Why?* and I've asked God a million times, "Why did You allow us to meet, knowing what the future held?" To this day I don't have an answer to those questions. I only know that although God does not tempt us, He does not prevent temptation from finding us. Larry and I were both sitting ducks, and the elephant danced all over our tail feathers. We were both in search of a Band-Aid. Simple as that. God would have delivered us from temptation, but we turned instead to each other. I own that.

Larry and I went our separate ways when the truth about our relationship surfaced, but the damage was done to one ministry and the two marriages that were crumbling before we met. Three and a half years later, when Larry and I married, we tried to put legs on something that was set in quicksand to begin with. Plus, I still didn't know why Steve and I were unable to find help from God and landed in divorce, so how was I supposed to believe God could help me with this new marriage?

And the elephant danced on. He danced around the table at Thanksgiving and around the tree at Christmastime.

And still, I remained silent.

One day after flushing one too many toilets and picking up a laundry basket full of wet, stinky towels, I snapped. I jumped on the back of the elephant and asked him to take me to the Nordstrom Anniversary Sale! Then on to the Half-Yearly Sale. And later he carried me to the Half-Yearly Shoe Sale and the Men's Half-Yearly Sale until Nordstrom Department Store became my home away from home. This all seemed fitting since our Nordstrom bill grew to be the size of an elephant!

I lived at South Coast Plaza.

Larry couldn't help but notice my change in behavior, because I'd never been a clothing hog before now. I'm known to wear the same pair of Levi's 501 button-fly jeans for three days in a row before washing them, only to wear them again for the next three. Designer racks have never called out to me, but now they screamed at the top of their lungs. I was a walking advertisement for Donna Karan, Calvin Klein, and Guess. When Larry'd see me coming through the back door with Nordstrom sacks up to my elbows, his question was always the same.

"Hey, Hon. What's up?"

"The Nordstrom charge card is what's up," I was tempted to say. Instead I said, "Not much. How was your day?"

My spending sprees were yet another form of acting out, just like the affair had been. I still didn't know how to speak up, stand up, and be direct about the truth of the matter and the truth about what mattered to me. So I bought things. But the shopping bags were bottomless. They couldn't fill my needs.

Neither Larry nor I knew what to do.

Larry's "What's up?" was just another way of saying "I don't know what to do" with what felt like an "I don't care."

I, on the other hand, shopped and shopped and shopped 'til I dropped. Literally.

After returning home from Nordstrom one February afternoon, I found myself curled up in a fetal position on the floor of our bedroom closet, crying my eyes out, buried under Nordstrom sacks. Larry soon found me there.

"Michele? Are you under there?"

"Leave me alone."

"Okay," Larry replied. "Uh, what's wrong with you?"

"What's wrong with me? What's wrong with me? I don't know, Larry! I don't know!" It was my turn, and I took it.

Sounding like a mother cow that lost her young, I bawled into a DKNY blouse with the tags still on it. I glared into the vacant eyes of my husband and continued my rant: "There, I said it! The perfect nonanswer I've heard a million times outta your mouth, and I got to say it first this time! I get it, Larry! I get it. It feels good to do nothing, to know nothing, to ignore everything! I beat you to the punch this time! What do you think about that? Huh? Huh? And don't you dare say 'I don't know'!"

He turned, gently closed the closet door, and tiptoed away.

I stayed in that closet like a traumatized pill bug and fell asleep. When I awoke, it was dark. I found my way to the light switch and flipped it on. "Lord, how on Earth did I get here, and where are You? I can't see You. I can't feel You. What can I do to fix this? What's my part in all of this? I can't get another divorce. I just can't."

Eat crow, Michele.

"Excuse me?" I questioned.

Eat crow. God said it again. I sat there bewildered, wondering if I finally had lost my mind. "Lord, I am eating crow. Platefuls of it. If I eat anymore, it'll come out my nose. I promise You, it will." I poured out my soul to God.

No. You're trying to pay for something I've already paid for. I listened further. *Share in my suffering, Michele. Serve them. Love them, and I will give you the power to do it. I suffered enough to carry you through yours.*

Then, like a warm embrace from a long-lost friend, hope wrapped itself around me. I hadn't felt hope in a very long time. I didn't have a clue as to what "eating crow" meant exactly, but I could see a tiny light at the end of my tunnel of despair. There seemed to be a plan again, one from beyond my closet, one I never could have found on my own.

God was asking me to work in silence, but His request felt nothing at all like the powerless voicelessness of my past. In my "previous life," good, important people like my ex-husband, the record label executives, and even those at church—people I desperately wanted and needed to get through to—were like stone figures standing around me. I didn't know how to move among them, to permeate their outer shells, no matter how hard I tried. The voice of reason would tell you that this new "eating crow" would feel more like working off an old debt, but it didn't. It was rooted in God's pure love for me and His plan of freedom for us. I didn't have to understand everything about it. God promised to make it work, and with so much at stake, I gave myself to it.

I hid God's plan in my heart—not for nobility's sake, but because I wasn't sure I could do it. But this peculiar new way of doing things brought with it strength and power, and it put a smile on my face I seemed unable to wipe off.

I had a secret. A good one that God Himself had whispered to me.

So, I was tireless. I washed sinks full of dishes, flushed toilets full of you-know-what, and even though on the receiving end of ill comment after ill comment, I skipped through the darts unscathed. Trying to pay for my offenses had just about killed me, but sharing in the suffering of my Lord felt like rising from the grave and kicking off my grave clothes. It was nothing less than a miracle. To me it was right up there with the parting of the Red Sea and raising Lazarus from the dead.

My trips to Nordstrom became a thing of the past, and so did the balance on our Nordstrom account.

After months of eating crow, my soul felt nourished, and I

had a spring in my step, even though I saw little to no change in my family. As I'm apt to do, I began questioning God again. "Did I hear You correctly? Am I doing this right? How much more of this stuff do I have to eat? Send reinforcements! Help!" These questions were sure signs I was losing my appetite for humble pie, and that frightened me. If I couldn't (or worse yet, *wouldn't*) do what I'd been asked to do, where would that leave me? What would become of the plan for my family?

It was Valentine's Day. I was feeling lower than low and needed to think, to regroup. I wanted to go shopping, but Nordstrom was off limits. I had weaned myself down to the cosmetic department at our local Target store. I couldn't do much damage there. Aisle 3 was my favorite, with ten gazillion lipsticks, eye shadows, and the latest, greatest nail polish colors of the season. The aisle had a heavenly glow about it with lights and mirrors designed to make a girl look ten years younger than she is. Luminescent, 3-D gel-photos of stars and supermodels (real enough to speak and blink) lined the cases and made me believe I could be as beautiful as they are. It was the perfect place to refill and refresh. I would need to visit Aisle 10 for the super-size package of toilet paper, but I tried not to think about that. I enjoyed a good hour visiting with Catherine Zeta-Jones at the Revlon case and Rene Russo over at Cover Girl. When I hit my quota of items like Brunette Bombshell nail polish and Tempest Blue eye shadow, I hippity-hopped toward Aisle 10 to stock up on TP.

Without warning, my shopping cart hung a sharp left and turned down Aisle 7, as if it had a mind of its own. I always avoided Aisle 7. The mere smell of it made my teeth ache and hips swell. Aisle 7 housed bag after bag of candy and cookies of every variety, and it was usually riddled with screaming children begging their mothers for what they couldn't live without, so I always steered clear of it. But this day I didn't have a choice, so I followed my cart's leading, and that's when I saw it—the display of all displays, erected by God Himself! One that offered me more help than Catherine Zeta-Jones and Rene Russo put together.

One might say I'd earned this architectural marvel that stood before me. Another might say I needed it more than makeup and TP. But I think it was more like the loaves and fishes Jesus multiplied to feed the five thousand,[1] or maybe I'd "paid it forward" when I was nine. I'm not sure. What couldn't be argued was that it was fifteen feet tall, blinding red, and had been erected in my honor!

"Sweets for the Sweet!" "Say it with LOVE!" "From His Heart to Hers." These and other slogans encircled a mountain of what looked like ten thousand bags of M&Ms! And not just any old M&Ms. We're talkin' God's M&Ms! All of them were red ones, just like the one I saved for God under my bed as a kid!

You're doing just fine, Michele. Keep eating crow. I'll turn it to chocolate, every single time. God's words rushed through my pounding heart.

My chin hit the floor, and so did my purse. Everything in it spilled out and rolled in every direction. I fell to my knees but not to pick up my belongings. I fell to my knees in relief, in awe and wonderment, and stared up at the bright red hope God built just for me. It was as if He saved that single red M&M from under my bed, tucked it in His pocket, and waited until now to multiply it by the thousands.

"Thank you" was all I could utter. I dabbed my tears and filled my cart with bag after bag of red M&Ms. The Mars Company marketing team thought they'd created a nice Valentine's display to sell lots of candy. Little did they know they were mere pawns in the hand of God for my encouragement.

I gathered myself and my belongings, grabbed an eighteen-roll pack of TP from Aisle 10, and returned to Aisle 3. One by one, I put back every cosmetic I'd chosen just minutes before. I didn't need them today. I had everything I needed in my cart: toilet paper and a gazillion red M&Ms.

When I got home I sneaked in through the back door like I had so many times before when smuggling in Nordstrom bags. This time it felt so good, so right, so powerful. I hid red M&Ms every place around the house I knew nobody would find them. I hid them behind the towels, under beds, and in my shoes. I even hid them behind the Charmin for good measure. If Larry found them now and then, I told him I was hiding them from myself. There was a lot of truth in that excuse. Every time I needed help eating crow, I rummaged through the house until I found a bag and popped a handful. And God did just as He promised. With every bite of crow, He turned it into chocolate.

This went on for a long time, and just when I was running low on M&Ms, my stepdaughter took a bite of crow! She stood up for me—right in front of everyone. Then, without notice, Travis took a bite, and soon Larry jumped in and ate a plateful by kindly asking the kids to pick up their wet towels and to keep their negative opinions to themselves. "You don't have to eat what's on your plate, but the rest of us would like to eat in peace," he said. I never heard another critical word about my cooking after that.

The elephant got the sniffles and soon after fell gravely ill. Seriously weakened, his dancing calmed to a gentle waltz, which made it a lot easier to keep from being stepped on.

Then one day, Cyndie did something that made my bites

of crow look like a single petit four. Larry and I had hit another rough patch. (I think it was the elephant's doing.) Larry jumped aboard the beast and trotted down to the courthouse to file for a divorce! I kept popping handfuls of crow, mucking up elephant dung and praying like crazy. I thought, "We made it this far— and now this?" I understood Larry's feelings more than he knew. I'd wanted to bolt a million times along the way, but now I felt strong and was thankful we'd never fallen weak at exactly the same time. In walked the grace-filled hand of Cyndie. Unbeknownst to me, she invited Larry out to lunch. I'm sure it went something like, "Hey, let's grab a bite 'n catch up." Absence of malice and all.

She had me on the ropes. Cyndie could have said myriad things to finish off Larry and me while sipping her iced tea, and few would have faulted her for it. It could have sounded something like, "We all knew this marriage would never last, Larry," or "What goes around comes around." Instead, she listened to Larry. She listened to his heart, and as she did she came to her own conclusions. Those conclusions prompted one question and—instead of playing the card of revenge—Cyndie asked Larry, "Do you want to divorce Michele?" "Ah, no," Larry answered. And with her next two words, Cyndie downed more crow than I had the entire time: "Then don't."

Those two words were all it took to talk Larry off the ledge. Just two words. Those two words, "Then don't." The minute they left Cyndie's mouth, the elephant keeled over and died, deader than a doornail, and that was the end of our intrusive, uninvited houseguest.

How a woman finds it in her heart to save the relationship that once annihilated her own can only be explained by the fact that God lives in her heart, big and strong. No other explanation makes any good sense.

On May 15, 2011, Cyndie took her last breath on Earth and her first deep, cancer-free breath in heaven. I was there when she did. Cyndie rose to glory with the same dignity she'd walked in for a little more than sixty years on Earth. I loved her and I miss her. I'll forever be thankful for our love and respect for each other. I still wear a bracelet she gave me years ago with 1 Corinthians 13 engraved deep into the sterling silver: "And of these three, Faith, Hope and Love, the greatest is Love." But that bracelet isn't the sweetest gift she gave me. The sweetest gift was the two words she uttered to Larry that helped preserve our marriage in 2000.

I wish I could tell you that eating crow became obsolete in our family but that's not how it played out. All families make mistakes. We hurt the ones we love but those who eat crow, no matter the cost, make it through to the finish line. The plain truth is, this exercise of humility, the one coined "eating crow," must be a unanimous effort by all parties. Uneaten crow is powerless.

Just about the time readers would be discovering *Untangled* in bookstores, I found myself holding divorce papers—again. And this time, I was eating crow alone. As hard as it was, I had to accept the wall of resistance and silence separating the two of us. When I couldn't scale it, break through it, or even make a small chip in it, I let go of my marriage. Some walls are simply impermeable. I never believed this to be true until I lived it. My job was to make every honest effort possible to keep channels of communication open between Larry and me until God released me to stop trying. When that sad day arrived, it was as if God was saying, "Enough is enough."

We never know what tomorrow will bring. It's probably best we don't. Security, even a false security, can be snatched away in

. instant. Relationships are deepened or lost in milliseconds of choices: to give or to deny, to nurture or to withhold, to forgive or to dig in with heels of self-righteousness and human will. God is a Gentleman and gives us a choice in these matters of the heart.

I lost them all: my husband, stepchildren, step-grand-children, step-in-laws, cousins, and even some of my closest friends. Looking back, I can't help but wonder if any of them were ever really mine to begin with.

Was I embarrassed? Like you can't imagine.

Heartbroken? Yes. But with time, God took the sorrow away.

Frightened? There were days during the eighteen-month divorce process when fear paralyzed me beyond the ability to lift my head up from my pillow. But through that fear I learned much about God's power to make final decisions in these fright-ening circumstances. God became my Abba. And I became a prayer warrior. There were days when prayer was the only thing I had and I soon learned it was the only thing I needed.

Divorce is a "game of the mind" on steroids. To preserve my sanity I had to "take captive every thought to make it obedient to Christ," as the apostle Paul instructs us in 2 Corinthians 10:5. As the months ticked by, I got pretty good at wielding God's promises to quench the fear and doubt before they took root in my heart.

True freedom for me was discovering that God is bigger than the onslaught of divorce. He has things for me to do even though my life is riddled with divorce. He's given me life and I will trust Him with every layer of it, as imperfect as some layers are. We tend to dwell on our failures and feel unworthy to do God's work, but I can't find scriptural support for giving up on serving God.

I gave my life to Christ in 1973 and it's not mine to take back, especially now. It's not mine to give up on and not mine to decide what I'm worthy of. I've learned to live with the embarrassment of divorce and also learned that it does not define me. Embarrassment is just an emotion; it has nothing to do with who I am in Christ. And when the voice of doubt tries to silence me, I laugh in its face and think, *What a weak move!* My God has been faithful to me in spite of my missteps!

But even still, do take caution, young lovers.

Be careful of your beginnings for they can never be rewritten. Wait for God's best for you, even when you don't want to wait. Especially when you don't want to. The more desperate we are to find love, the more prone we are to accept less than God has for us. Desperation leads to failure. Overboard enthusiasm at the start of a relationship often leads to overcontrol later on.

What begins in the flesh doesn't often end in the Spirit.

And your words—they are powerful. Unkind words are like feathers blowing in the wind from a pillow that's been split at the seams. They can never be retrieved. They can only be forgiven. And isolation, choosing to withhold words from those around you, is the cruelest form of communication of all.

Yet, kind words, words from God's own heart, are like the healing balm of Gilead.[2] They are alive. They move, heal, and breathe life into places where the stench of death has choked out love—places where life and love have been destroyed and stolen. God's healing words restore what the locusts have eaten.[3]

Choose your words carefully, especially in the valley of pain, for the fruit of your words will remain long after you've moved on. And choose this day, life not death, blessings not curses that you might live.[4]

Above all else, we have to continue to love with *all* our hearts, no matter what, in order to live. We must forgive. Blame and bitterness will kill everything that follows. Let's pray for peace to flood our minds.

That's how God pulled me through time and time again and always will.

And what part did the Beatles and chocolate play in this sacred trifecta? Well, when I was nine years old, Paul McCartney told me he wanted to hold my hand, nothing more. He and God were on exactly the same page, only I didn't listen to either of them.

I didn't listen when I dated Jim and became pregnant in 1973 or when I turned a deaf ear in 1984 and fell for Larry. The Beatles tried to set a standard for me I wish I'd set for myself but didn't have the guts, wisdom, or maturity in God to set. I paid dearly.

Now I keep a Bible, a bowl of M&Ms, and a copy of *Meet the Beatles* within arm's reach to remind me that God is bigger than my mistakes, that chocolate heaped over humble pie is a healing force, and that Paul McCartney was right: I don't have to give anyone anything more than my hand to find true love. If only I'd believed him . . .

Chapter 6

IN SEARCH OF THE INVISIBLE MAN
untangling the knot of fatherlessness

———

Year: 1976 and 1986 / **Age:** 21 and 31
Place: the Hillhead Beach house and Pam's office, years later

As soon as I began dialing his number, my hand started arguing with my heart. Then my head scolded both of them, *Hush! Just do it. It's the right thing to do! Isn't this what a good daughter does on Father's Day?* I reasoned with myself.

My roommate Cac, with the best of intentions, suggested I call my dad before the day slipped away. And why wouldn't she? She'd been given the gift of a wonderful father who was there for her every day of her life. Well, until recently that is. On this Father's Day, of all Father's Days, Cac would gladly pay AT&T a million dollars to get her dad on the phone, but that was impossible. Cac's dad had died of a heart attack last year while jogging down Beach Boulevard one sunny afternoon. He was just shy of his fiftieth birthday when the paramedics wheeled him into the ER as an unidentified DOA. Her dad, Maurice, never jogged with identification in his pocket. Why

UNTANGLED

would he? When the sun was starting to set, and he hadn't returned home, Cac's mom asked her to do the only thing that made any sense. "Call Westminster Hospital, Cathy, and ask if anyone's been brought in."

When Cac made the call, she knew her father had to be dead. If he had a single breath left in him, suffering from a twisted ankle or even a hit-and-run, he would have called home by now. That's how faithful he was. He was that reliable.

"Has anyone been brought into the emergency room? Unidentified?" Cac asked the receptionist and closed her eyes to receive the blow of a lifetime. "You and your family need to come down here right away," the nurse recommended.

It seemed so unfair to all of us who had less-than fathers. "Why did she have to lose hers?" I asked God that question more times than I could count. It would have been impossible for me to lose my dad, even if he jogged straight down the centerline of Beach Boulevard in rush-hour traffic every single day of his life. You can't lose something you never had.

Against my better judgment, I dialed the first three digits of my dad's number. *You're only gonna get hurt again.* The practical-protective-adult side of me tried its best to save me. But what daughter doesn't wish beyond all hopes for a father's love, care, protection, advice, and a million other things—even though she's never gotten any of them? Well, that's not entirely true. I knew he loved me if in word only, because he said it every single time we were together. And he was kind to me, generally speaking. But actions speak louder and more precisely than words. So when months on end passed by with no sign of him, I came to the sad conclusion that either he didn't know how to love, or I was just plain unlovable. As a kid, I always naturally believed the latter. When he did come around, I clung to him like glue and bent his ear with a long, exaggerated list of the spectacular things going on in my life.

Maybe he'll want to be a part of your life if your life is more exciting, Michele! A voice inside coached me, like a stage mother. But as quickly as he came, he always went away, and none of my improvisational monologues had the power to make him want to stay.

As his little sports car drove away into the night air, my long list of excuses kicked in to cover for him. *He's busy. Mother has pitted him against us. His father coddled him to the point of emotional atrophy, helplessness, and dependency, all so that Dad would never leave the family business and would forever have the propensity to move back in with his father for safety. That's why he's weak and invisible. That's why he never follows through, Michele. Poor dad. Poor us.* Poor excuses.

"R-r-ring . . . ring . . . ring . . . ring." Dad's phone rang one time for every ten beats of my heart. And right when I was ready to skip the idea altogether, Dad picked up.

"Hello?" he said.

I took a deep breath. "Hey, Dad. It's me (awkward pause) . . . Michele."

"Oh. Hi, Shelly!" he replied with the believability of a great actor. His love and excitement sounded so real; I wanted to feel what Cac would feel, if only for part of a moment. I wanted to pretend I had a real be-there dad who could offer me up a conversation, warm and lasting, full of words fat with faithfulness. That's what I was listening for. But in my heart of hearts I knew better. Nevertheless, the sound of Dad's voice filled my heart to the brim. But his script had baggage so heavy the plane never got off the ground. And within seconds he wanted to hang up. He needed to go do this or that, and my ears stopped listening.

At this point his voice sounded just like Miss Othmar's, Linus' beloved teacher from the *Peanuts* comic strip, who talked to him in her "wha-wha-wha's." But the difference between Miss Othmar and my dad was that Linus could understand his teacher's gibberish. And Miss Othmar was there for Linus every day when he arrived at school.

Dad was never around for me, and his frantic words on the other end of the phone said the same thing to me every time: "Everything is more important to me than you, Michele."

"I sure love you! I hope you know that! Gotta run now, you take care, beautiful. Say hi to Mom and the girls for me," he rattled off. That, being translated, means, "Wha-wha. Wha-wha-wha-wha."

Besides that, the "click" was coming, just around the corner. I knew it. The sound produced when the phone's receiver hits the rock-hard base is not just the sound of plastic against plastic, it is the saddest sound in all the world. It was to me, anyway. It was the sound of my dad walking out of my life one more time. I hated the click. I hated the walking out more. The click said more than all of Dad's "wha-wha's" put together; it rang in my ears for days, months . . . even years.

"Happy Father's Day, Dad." I said it, knowing the click was coming any second. "Thank you, Shelly! That's right. It is Father's Day, isn't it?" he said. And the fact that he hadn't remembered the holiday commemorating fathers everywhere only served to remind me that he attached no importance to the job of being a father. But then why would he? My dad was adopted at infancy by a man who was anything but nurturing, and by a woman who was as mean as a snake. Just because one decides to birth or adopt a child or two doesn't qualify them as good parents.

So much of my dad's life seemed mysterious. Who was he? Where did he come from? Some said he looked Italian, while others thought he was Spanish. Why did his real parents let him go? Did they have to or want to? Why weren't we allowed to talk about his adoption?

They say that the apple doesn't fall far from the tree. The Bible puts it in more sobering terms in Exodus 20:5 when it tells us that the sins of the father will be visited upon his children and his children's children to the third and fourth generations. But what happens when you don't know where on Earth your family tree resides? And since my dad had two fathers, one adopted and the other natural, does that mean he had apples falling from two trees, so to speak, and from multiple generations? Unfortunately, I think the answer is yes. But that doesn't mean God punished my dad for the sins of his fathers and forefathers. But he did eat the tainted apples that fell from family trees, as did his fathers and forefathers. To rise above his lineage, Dad would've needed an insatiable hunger for God's help. Sadly, he didn't.

So, where did that leave me? Was I subject to fallen apples I couldn't see, inspect, or understand? I was born into a bottom-less barrel of fallen apples. The evidence of this was all around me, playing out in both my mother and my father. I was born to an invisible father who, himself, was born to invisible fore-fathers. It made a strange kind of sense to me, even as a young woman dialing the phone on Father's Day. But what to do about it? I had no idea.

Because I didn't know my father very well or what made him tick, I couldn't possibly know who I was. So my situation seemed not only illusive but insurmountable.

I think "invisible" is almost more painful than yardsticks and coat hangers against the back. Although, now that I've had the chance to meet people from all kinds of places and back-grounds who are still suffering from acts of violence their fathers, uncles, and others inflicted upon their innocent bodies, I may need to stand corrected on this point. What I do know is this: physical abuse is an action, an effort. It leaves a mark behind as evidence that something happened. Emotional abuse leaves clear scars behind that can be retraced, tackled, and healed.

But "invisible" leaves nothing tangible to show for its stealth. You walk away wondering, *What just happened?* You ache in places no one has ever touched or bothered with. You walk away worthless, and as far as you know, you dreamed the whole thing up. You walk away wishing you could have done something to make it better. And you walk away the fool for believing in the mirage called a loving family.

Was it generations of invisible, rotten apples that ruined my chances to have a father? Was it the sins of faceless people I'd never met, that even he'd never met? Was my father really my father at all? If not for physical characteristics like my eyes, nose, and cheekbones, I'd wonder who fathered me. I'd wonder if I was adopted as well.

"Yeah, Dad. It's Father's Day," I answered, filling in the blanks for him. I went on, "I wanted to wish you a happy Father's Day. What will you do today?"

"Oh, you know me, Shelly. I'll play tennis like I do every day. In fact, wow, look at the clock! I'm running late for my match down at the club. I've really gotta go, Honey. Bye," he said.

And then, there it was. Proof that telephones can make sad sounds. Evidence that fathers don't have to walk out a door of your house to abandon you. Alexander Graham Bell made it so very easy for Dad. With one crashing blow of plastic against plastic, he walked away, again.

Click.

"Sure, Dad. I understand," I answered to a dial tone. I pulled the phone away from my ear and stared at it. The tears welled up faster than I could pull them back inside. The click came so quickly this time I didn't even have the chance to form a decent lump in my throat. The lump was my friend. It held back my tears so Dad wouldn't know. This time I didn't need the lump. He was gone quicker than even I could imagine.

Somehow I knew better than to show signs of sadness to my dad. It was the same gut instinct that coached me to go on and on to him about my accomplishments. I didn't want to lose the remnant of the father I held in my little hand. One thing is certain: I learned early how to cover for people in my life. I was a little chameleon who changed colors when my mom hit me and again when my dad left me to deal with my mother all alone. I covered for their alcohol abuse too. And I was really good at it. Sadly, that meant I was really bad at taking good care of myself.

One day, in my faraway future, I would find and grab hold of the tangled thread around that chameleon's neck and yank its little head off. But until then, the colorful lizard was a pretty handy Band-Aid.

"A difference which makes no difference is no difference." It took this bit of pointy-eared wisdom from the Vulcan Spock to spit the hard truth in my face. Spock opened my eyes to why I never talked "real" to my dad. It wouldn't have made one iota of difference. Dad couldn't give me what he hadn't been given, and neither could my mother.

Without realizing it, I confused God's character with those of my fractured parents' and left the door wide open for the accuser to come along and convince me of lies like the one that seemed so true right now: *Tonight's a good night to swallow a bunch of sleeping pills, 'cause God isn't happy with you anyway.* Or a million other lies about who we are, who we'll never be, and what God thinks about that. And in my case, because my earthly father's words were unreliable, I found it nearly impossible to trust in God's promises or even relate to Him as a father.

Jesus was easy for me to relate to. Mankind whipped God's Son to within an inch of His life. I could relate to that kind of injustice. I was drawn to Jesus like a magnet. But Jesus also came that we might see and know His Father, the One who sent Him. "Anyone who has seen me has seen the Father."[1] That verse felt utterly impossible for me to relate to. Yet, somewhere deep within me I knew if Jesus could live in me to forgive, guide, and change me, He could also be trusted in the promises I couldn't grasp. Who was this Father Jesus spoke of so fondly, so wanted me to know? I hoped I'd know Him one day. I hoped I'd be comfortable in His presence one day. In the meantime, the Word of God often fell flat when it spoke about the Father. But even in the midst of this confusion, God the Father had a plan for me.

After my sleeping pill stint in '84, it took little to no time for me to find the thread in the tangled ball that was attached to my dad's mysterious heritage. When I gave that thread a tug, it didn't budge and felt like it was looped around every other thread in my life. When I pulled on it again, it seemed to go all the way down to the center of the ball. I sensed that Jesus and I would do well with another set of hands to loosen it, so I called the person God had already used to help me untangle other threads. I called Pam Rice, my very gifted counselor.

"Hi, Michele." Pam answered the phone in that cheerful voice of hers.

"I need to see you again," I said.

"Yep, it's probably time for us to get down to the next layer, Michele," Pam said, in a tone full of pure assurance, hope, and comfort.

"You have such a gift, Pam," I said.

"I watch what Jesus can do for people who come to this office every day, Michele. I would never think of going into the trenches without Him," Pam replied.

"It all seems so simple to you, Pam," I said.

"It is, Michele. People's brokenness falls into but a few categories. Once a person realizes how common their issues are, even though the pain would tell them otherwise, it's more reasonable for them to believe that God is just waiting to heal them. There's no test or temptation that's beyond the course of what others have had to face, and God will never let them down.[2] That's who He is, Michele, the Redeemer. I hear the same stories every day all wrapped up in different circumstances," Pam explained.

I said nothing and drank in the truth of the Truth. "Why can't we talk about these deep things at church?" I asked her.

"Because it scares people to open up to others. They are afraid they will be judged, rejected, condemned, or thought less of if they don't yet have the victory in every area of their lives. When we admit we are still in the process of healing, many people don't know what to do with that. They think it makes Jesus look bad if we are not all perfect and healed. But God is the Redeemer all the way through the process, Michele, and it is a process. And sometimes what people don't understand scares them. Most people don't know how to handle their own emotions, so it makes them uncomfortable when they are confronted with the raw pain in someone else. God the Father is not afraid of our emotions. He is the only One who truly understands them and doesn't judge or condemn us for our emotions but wants to bring healing to them."

I understood that one. Being "the good little girl" was the role I always felt the most comfortable playing. Before 1984, when my Christian friends shared their problems with me, I was quick to judge and wondered why they couldn't just get it together. Little did I know that pride comes before a fall, and I was right around the corner from the biggest stumble of my life.

I never relished the thought of going to Pam for help. In fact, I'd often come up with a million reasons why I needed to cancel on her. But every time I went, although I felt unclothed, I never felt naked. Humility and admission of what was still hurting and why I was so angry about it always ushered in healing, peace, and a new understanding about who God really is in contrast to who I thought He was before that day. And most of these twisted threads could be traced back to things I learned from my earthly father and from the teacher of human, conditional love.

"See you tomorrow at 3:00, Michele." As always, Pam prayed before we hung up the phone, and I knew that once again God would join Pam and me in her office the next day, just as He always did.

"This is going to take work, Michele." These were Jesus' words to me on the twin bed in 1984. This job of untangling threads in my life was more work than I ever imagined it would be.

The next day Pam asked me about my father. And then she did what she always does. She explained how we learn our worth, our security, and sense of safety and trust from our fathers. "If that doesn't happen," Pam explained, "we spend the rest of our lives trying to find our worth in accomplishments and are attracted to flawed partners who look exactly like our fathers. We're trying to rewrite a happy ending, Michele. But we only find rejection and further disappointment. We have to stop projecting onto our heavenly Father what our earthly fathers were like. God the Father is the source of all love, mercy, and compassion and not like any human being we've ever known. Only trusting and knowing the true God can give us the ending we are looking for."

"What do we do? What can I do to change this?" I asked.

Pam said, "We look at our fathers for who they were and who they were not. We don't stop there in blame and excuses, but we look at how they differ from God the Father. We speak, within the walls of this office, the truth about what our dads did to us, what we believe about ourselves because they were not the fathers we wanted or needed them to be. And even if we are angry with God for allowing all the hurt, rejection, or abuse in our lives, we need to vent that anger and disappointment as well. And after we've cried enough tears to let it all out, we ask God to give us the power to forgive our dads. And to give us the grace to hold God blameless. Not that God needs our forgiveness, but we need to be honest with Him. We need to let Him know how all our past hurts have affected us and tainted our ability to fully trust Him and see if there is any resentment in our hearts toward Him. And then we ask for one more thing. We ask God to break the patterns of our fathers and their fathers and their fathers. Of our mothers and their mothers. And we ask God to give us a new future and a new hope to pass down to the future generations."

Before Pam and I prayed, she asked me to close my eyes. She asked God to give me a mental picture of what He was doing for me to heal my father-wounds. I sat quietly with closed eyes, wondering if anything would come to mind. The minutes felt long and uncomfortable as I sat waiting for something to pop into my head. Pam waited patiently, for she knew that God would come through. I stilled my heart and breathed to calm my nerves.

I waited on the Lord.

The first thing I saw was a pasture with a beautiful white horse grazing in the spring meadow. Then I saw a large oak-like tree in the middle of the field, but it was anything but beautiful. In fact, it was dead. It was as if the surrounding scenery was painted in full watercolors, but the tree was penned in black and white. It didn't have one leaf on its brittle branches. I saw Jesus walk out from behind the tree, and He was holding the hand of a nine-year-old little girl. She was pretty, well-kempt, and she had my smile. She was wearing a crisp, white cotton dress. Her hair was soft and clean, as were her knees, legs, and feet. Her little bangs were cut straight, and they looked nothing like mine did when I was her age. She beckoned me to come closer, so I walked toward them. When I got close enough to touch them both, Jesus took me by the hand. I could see that the little girl was me, and she was about the age I was when my father left me for the last time.

Jesus touched the tree, and from the bottom of the trunk upward, the tree came to life in full color. Leaves sprang out on every branch, in every direction, thick and glossy green. He touched the tree again, and fruit popped out all over it, so much that the branches sagged from the weight. As I looked closer, I saw that the fruit was of every variety imaginable. Peaches, nectarines, pears, apples, and even grapes hung down in big clusters all over this gorgeous tree. And not one piece of fruit fell to the ground.

Jesus lifted up the "little me" so I could pick a piece of fruit and eat it. And so I did! Giggling the whole time, I devoured bite after bite, until the juice was dripping off my little chin and running down my neck. I stood there watching this beautiful picture of new life and abundance. I felt healing welling up from the depths of my soul. Jesus held the "little me" in the crook of

His elbow, and as I finished eating to my content, Jesus smiled at the "adult me," and I whispered the words "Thank You."

Jesus sat with us under the tree and talked about His Father and our Father being one and the same. For the first time, I really wanted to know this Father of His. He didn't feel mysterious or distant to me. And I didn't feel alone, without . . . fatherless.

I opened my eyes and told Pam about what I'd just seen. Pam threw me that knowing smile that comes only from experiencing God's handiwork.

The promise of Psalm 68:5 became my motto, that God is the Father to the fatherless, and getting to know Him—the Good Father, that is—has filled my life to overflowing.

I never again felt sad at the thought of my earthly father. I'm thankful that his imperfections drew me straight to God my Father and all He has become to me. He's shown me His romantic side—when He answers little prayers that would mean absolutely nothing to anyone else but mean everything to me. I've seen His protective side—on icy highways and snow-covered roads at night. And I've seen His impeccable timing and management skills as He opens and closes the doors of my goals and dreams, all for my benefit. Knowing and being comfortable with God the Father has helped me in so many ways but none more than in my role as a wife and mother. Without it, I would ask more of my husband than he can give and would likely teach my children to find their security in people instead of God.

The sins of the father may pass through to the third and fourth generations, but God's blessings are passed to a thousand generations![3] By my calculations that's about thirty thousand years.

"I and the Father are one."[4] I understand that now. I enjoy that now. I embrace the whole Godhead. Its mystery and majesty no longer confound me. Things once tangled in the roots of my ignorance have been cut loose to understanding. I see it through a glass dimly, yet sharp enough to allow the Father's love to envelop me. God shreds pages in our family's history books to write new chapters beyond what we can author! To us, such things seem impossible. To God, it's mere child's play.

Chapter 7

RALPH
untangling the knot around boundary lines

———

Year: 1992 / **Age:** 37
Place: in the back hills scrub oak of Canyon Country, California

*F*ortuity was kind to us that day. A soft summer breeze blew and carried with it shards of leaves, earth, and destiny that bit our necks, forearms, and faces. He closed his eyes and a single tear fell short of washing the sting away. He was asking for my hand, so I—without hesitation or foresight of consequence— leaned in to him and brushed away the pain. He opened his eyes and out poured nothing less than deep love and gratitude. That was the first time I touched Ralph and the first time I was close enough to memorize the sweet smell of his skin, a smell that to this day remains etched in my memory . . . that of lavender, dandelion, and wild mint leaves. Of course, that would be his cologne of choice. What else would it be? He pegged me for a girl who likes an elegant, rough-and-tumble kind of guy. On the one hand, he was everything I'd ever dreamed of. On the other hand, he was nothing less than pure danger.

I remember it all like it was yesterday, the way he took my

breath away. His black-brown eyes pierced my soul, and right then and there I knew I'd never be the same.

Hold on, girl. Don't let him see ya sweat, I told myself and tried to still my pounding heart. I'd learned long ago to hold my cards close to the vest with guys like this, but he was different. I couldn't hide from him. I couldn't fool him, not for a second. I was done for. He knew it, and so did I. He sensed my undefined fear. You see, my streetwise friend Diane told me he'd been known to push girls like me around. *So why the big attraction?* That was the question I still couldn't answer as I stood dangerously close to this dish of a guy.

Drowning in pure attraction, my emotions were running away with me like a herd of wild horses. He offered up a soft "Hello" in that deep, warm voice of his, and my poker face broke. I heard myself sigh out loud, and I tried to take it back, but it was too late. He took a step toward me, and I surrendered a smile with the hope of melting his heart, returning the favor. Maybe then I could regain my composure.

How did I find him, or did he find me? And, am I enough for him? Can I handle him? Can he be tamed? Should I run like the wind, knowing he'll bolt at the drop of a hat? Or should I trust my heart? Is he my "Once Upon a Time" or my worst nightmare?

Yes, I remember every second of our first encounter like it was yesterday. And then came today. How could everything feel so right one minute and go so horribly wrong the next?

I think my first mistake was thinking that my love for him was strong enough to change him. I've heard the rogue side of a male can be traced back five or more generations. He and I came from two different worlds, two very different bloodlines. Those two worlds were bound to collide at some point, and when they did—oh, how the fur flew!

My second mistake was thinking Cinderella could come through for me. 'Rella made me believe that pumpkins can become carriages pulled by horses that magically appear where mice once stood and could carry me away to the land of "Happily Ever After." Well, 'Rella was dead wrong. My prince was born with two left feet. He stepped on my toes and pushed me too far on this hot summer day, and there were no soft breezes blowing this time to wipe away the tears. The only thing blowing was my lid, along with sweat, dust, and deep disappointment.

I kicked, he groaned. I kicked him in the gut again, and he spun around and tried to kick me back. But I backed him into a corner and had him over a barrel. I kept my body close to his in such a way as to make it impossible for him to retaliate. "Keep your enemies closer" was the mantra my instincts called upon as I reared back my boot and kicked him one more time. He wilted and stared at me as if to say "I give." But I wasn't finished with him yet. A woman's scorn is an ugly thing. I never dreamed I was capable of such, but self-preservation is a God-given gift. I pulled him up by the collar and slugged him as hard as I could, square in the jaw. Blood flew through the air like a Rain Bird sprinkler. Not his blood—mine. One of his teeth sliced my knuckle to the bone. Adrenaline deadened the pain.

This bully found an ancient button inside of me and pushed it when he threw me down moments earlier. His attack gave me the fuel I needed to work him over. Little did he know I spent the first eleven years of my life being beaten to a pulp by both my mom and my sister Marilyn. Time after time, Marilyn waltzed into my bedroom, came up from behind, and just started swinging. With every punch she told me, "If ya hit me back, I'll hit you again, twice as hard." And I believed her. When she was done getting her ya-yas out on my eighty-five-pound body, she turned and walked out of my room like it was all my fault, like I deserved it. I lived under her tyranny until the day I'd had all I could take, closed my eyes, and started swinging back. I can still feel the connection of my fist meeting bone and soft tissue. When I opened my eyes, Marilyn was long gone and never touched me again. That's where I was with this guy Ralph today. A sweet, quirky name for a big, fat bully. But this time I was swinging with my eyes wide open.

The unraveling of Ralph and me had been coming for weeks. Everyone around us saw it before I did. Often I tried to speak my peace, and Ralph's comeback was always the same, "What *is* your problem? Get off my back!" I'd shrink like a snail and try a different set of words the next day. The truth was I didn't know how to ask, so Ralph didn't bother to listen.

Being ignored was one of the many injustices I'd learned to live with, but earlier today Ralph digressed to an all-new low, one I couldn't live with. He flung me down with the force of his weight behind it. I landed in a pile and smashed my knee against a wooden post, cracking my kneecap. With head hung low, I limped away to lick my wound, when—in a flash—thirty-seven years of being afraid of my own shadow melted into hot molten "I've had it!" and I did an about-face and executed the aforementioned walloping with blood, sweat, and tears flying everywhere.

We were both guilty. I, guilty of trusting Walt Disney. Ralph, guilty to the bone of one thing and one thing only: of being an animal. Equus, to be specific, or as most humans would call him: a horse.

Ralph, my very first horse, was a birthday gift the day I turned thirty-seven. His registered name was Zaliant Prince, and his family tree was diseased just like mine. I think that's why I was attracted to him to begin with. We picked up the sixteen-hand, twelve-hundred-pound hooligan for a song. That should have been our first clue that something was awry with this bargain-basement birthday present. The seller gave us some hard-luck story about how she was being forced to sell the pinto gelding to feed her children.

The day Ralph arrived was one of the happiest days of my life. I didn't sleep for weeks and loved walking out to our make-shift pole barn to stare at the pretty boy in the middle of the night just to make sure I wasn't dreaming. He was big and hand-some, and he was mine, all mine.

I didn't know the first thing about riding a horse, so I made a few calls and found out who the trainer of choice was in our area of the canyon. It was the one, the only, Natasha! I gave Natty a call, and after she made me feel less than two inches tall, she reluctantly put me on her schedule for a 10:00 a.m. lesson, three days a week. "It's very difficult to teach a woman of your age to ride. Fear usually gets the better of her. But if anyone can pull it off, I can," she bragged.

"I'll show her. I'll learn to ride in no time," I assured friends and family in innocence even after the training bills began to pile up. And now, six months into it, I was nowhere near ready to break free from Natty. Ralph was eating my lunch in every les-son, and Natty described me as "a sack of potatoes draped over a saddle." I wanted to quit a hundred times over.

One day, while I was pouring myself into my riding breeches and hopping on one foot to pull on my boot, Larry asked me the question I'd been asking myself for weeks. "Are you sure you want to do this, Michele? You don't seem to have a natural apti-tude for riding. Maybe tennis or racquetball lessons would be a better fit."

Those were fightin' words. I was bound and determined to hang in there with Ralph and Natty, just to spite him.

But spite comes at a price. Right in the middle of my next lesson, Ralph did what Natty coined "the unforgivable sin." More simply put, he reared up. The minute his front feet lifted off the arena dirt three inches, Natty dismounted the big galoot, got in her red, oxidized Mercedes, and drove away, never to return. "I will not train a horse that chooses to rear!" were her exact words on my answering machine later that day.

Ralph and I were left standing in a cloud of dust with bits of gravel in our teeth from Natty's rear tires. "What's the big deal?" I asked Ralph. He said nothing. So I jumped aboard and decided to give it a go on my own. "We don't need that hoity-toity trainer, Ralph," I said, and legged him into a trot. It took Ralph a grand total of five minutes to figure out that Lil' Miss Know-It-All was no longer watching us. It was then he tossed me into next week and broke my kneecap. That's when I socked him in the jaw and kicked him in the belly hard enough to knock the wind right out of him. I got back up in the saddle, broken knee and all, and trotted that thickheaded horse around and around until his tongue hung to the ground. Then I tied him to the same post he used to crack my knee on and left him there in ninety-degree heat for three hours to think about it.

Sitting on the couch with a bag of frozen peas on my knee gave me time to reflect on my journey with Ralph. It was a road that looked all too familiar. I had to admit it. The problem wasn't Ralph's; it was mine.

For as long as I could remember I was in intimate relationships that didn't work, so why did I think it would be different with Ralph? All my life I believed that my happiness lay in the hands of someone else. I gave more than my fair share and got less than I hoped for, every single time. I changed my colors and habits to fit the other person's needs and hadn't a clue of my own needs. I didn't respect myself, so why should they respect me? Ralph wasn't the first guy to call me on it, but he was the first one who forced me to listen. His correction was swift and clear. The day he slapped me on the wrist, or knee I should say, was the most honest confrontation anyone had ever dealt me.

There's nothing like a horse to call you on the carpet. Ralph had been walking all over me for months, and I had done nothing to stop him. I sat in the saddle in lesson after lesson as a mere passenger, hoping against hope that Ralph would do as I wished. But all the hoping in the world wasn't going to grant me my wishes. The day he broke my knee was the day he got tired of our silly little game of push and pull. He'd been around this block with countless riders, and that's why his last owner sold him to us. Little did the seller know she was doing me a great service. From the minute Ralph arrived at our farm, he began answering a list of lifelong questions I'd left unanswered for years. I finally got the message and had a bag of frozen peas on my knee to prove it.

Without help, I knew Ralph's next argument would most likely land me in the orthopedic ward at Mesa Community Hospital, so I called Bill Duer, the local cowboy horse whisperer.

"Sounds to me like we need to get you outta that arena and into the real world with ole Ralphie boy." Bill laughed long and hard as he listened to story after story of Ralph's antics. "A good old-fashioned trail ride will even out the playing field, Michele. But I gotta warn ya, I have one hard and fast rule: no matter what happens, you can't get off the horse."

My stomach did a somersault. Bill was right. It was time to learn to ride it out, and no one else could do my riding for me.

If I wanted to find the fairy tale, I was going to have to let go of the Cinderella fantasies about life and love. I was tired of dead-end relationships.

As soon as my knee healed up, Bill and I hit the trail. He rode a quiet quarter horse mare named Sadie, and I was on Ralph.

I was scared to death. Ralph was too. Our first big challenge was to slide down a four-foot drop at the edge of a dry riverbed. Bill went first. He asked his mare to sit back on her haunches and slide down the bank on her butt, then walk across the riverbed to the other side. He made it look so simple. I was so hoping Ralph would do as Sadie did, but just like old habits, old hopes die hard.

Ralph and I got to the edge, and he not only wouldn't go, but he reared up in protest. I could envision Natty's tire tracks etched in my driveway. I wanted to quit. I wanted to quit so badly.

Bill started barking out instructions. "Sit up, Michele! Whack him on the butt! Mean it! Keep him facing forward! Use your legs. He can't rear up if he's going forward! Don't let him think about it! Don't let him set his back feet! Kick his hindquarters out from under him, if ya have to!"

I don't know what ached more, my legs, my brain, my lungs, or my heart. Ralph was jumping and squirming like a bug in a cast-iron skillet. He spun around one more time and headed toward home!

"Get that horse back here, Michele!" Bill shouted.

I shortened my reins and pulled Ralph's nose around to my right foot, circled him and rode him back to the riverbank. I took a minute to catch my breath. "Are you sure I can't get down and just lead him across, Bill? The sun is going down." I begged. I pleaded. My reasoning fell on deaf ears.

For the next thirty minutes I did the best I could with everything Bill shouted at me. Driving a hard bargain felt so foreign to me. It was exhausting. I wanted to cry. I wanted to give up, give in, get off, and go home and take a hot bath with a chaser of Advil. But Bill's one-and-only rule kept me in the saddle. Just when I thought my legs couldn't squeeze another time, I looked down at where the bank had been, and it was gone. Ralph's endless dancing had obliterated it. There was nothing left to slide down. All we needed to do was to walk forward. He still wouldn't go.

I thought of the times I'd faced obstacles and when God moved the obstacle aside, I couldn't see past my fear and disbelief, thinking the obstacle was still there.

"Calm down, just walk forward, Michele," Bill said. (Or maybe it was God, I don't recall.)

I made the choice to obey. I focused past the obstacle and straight ahead to my teacher. I looked in the direction I wanted to go, popped Ralph on the butt one more time, and legged him forward. He walked across the riverbank and stood next to Sadie. Bill said, "Great! Now go back and do it again!"

"You've got to be kidding, Bill. It's dark out here!"

Bill gave me a look, and I walked Ralph back to point one, moved him over to a fresh spot, and asked him to slide. He sat back, and when the bank gave way beneath his front hooves, I gave him a swift kick and down the riverbank he slid! We did it! We did it in the dark of night! That was the first time Ralph learned that he could trust me even more than the eyes in his head. It was the first time I learned how to speak my mind and believe in the truth more than the darkness surrounding me. And Ralph didn't fault me for it, either. In fact, he respected me for it.

When I became the leader Ralph could count on, he did whatever I asked of him. I drew lines of self-respect in sandy riverbanks, over hilltops, and through scrub oak as high as Ralph's nose.

"Good boy, Ralph!" became my new confession. Inside my head I heard "Good girl, Michele." Confidence brought about clarity of mind and the ability to do what was right instead of reacting out of fear, need, and helplessness. Ralph's body relaxed under me, and it was obvious that even though encouragement was foreign to him, he loved hearing it as much as I loved giving it. I disciplined Ralph with my crop when he deserved it, but those times became few and far between. Every day I felt stronger inside, and Ralph carried me through wind and weather. I bathed him at the end of each ride and told him over and over what a great horse he was. His eyes grew soft and trusting, as did mine.

We learned to jump fences and rode with the hounds of the Hunt Club, but with age catching up with us, I felt Ralph's back begin to weaken. I called the vet to take a look-see, and he told me Ralph was fine. We took some time off, and when we started in again, I learned to hold his back together using my legs as a back brace. With my support, Ralph moved along pain free. It was hard work for both of us but well worth it, because we could keep on riding. He was comfortable and bright-eyed and rode with his beautiful chestnut-colored ears up and forward.

I sold horse supplements at horse shows and saved up enough money to compete in the 1993 Canadian National Championships with Ralph. We won a National Top Ten title. This was quite a feat for a girl who once sported a bag of frozen peas and cowered to her older sister. Whatever Ralph and I did, we took care of each other. We were better together than either one was alone.

After the nationals, Ralph's back took months to heal, and I knew it was time to retire my friend. Besides, I needed to close the book of fairy-tale endings and get back to living in the real world.

An unsung hero is defined as one who makes a substantive yet unrecognized contribution to another's life. Ralph will always be my unsung hero. He taught me never to ride for the ribbons or glory but to ride for truth and without fear, and the ribbons will follow. Ralph taught me to win from the inside out. He taught me to win for all the right reasons.

God has used horses, more than any other living being, to teach me what an honest relationship looks like. You can't lie to a horse. You can lie to yourself, your friends, your spouse, your kids, and even God, but it is virtually impossible to lie to a horse. Horses demand honesty and a pure heart. They ask that you listen more often than you speak. They will only obey if your demands are fair, trustworthy, and without ego. Anything less and they'll ride you harder than you'll ever ride them. They are quick to forgive, but if you try to control them with ill motive, they'll never forgive you. These are the laws of equus.

There are countless times in every lasting relationship when boundaries are tested and challenged to the uttermost. These challenges appear to be enemies at first glance, yet are friends who bring to the union gifts of width, breath, depth, and worth.

And then there's the Deep Winter. In this season the storms crash down upon the roof and walls of the relationship, and cold winds of doubt and fear blow in on its heels. The walls of love and respect buckle to the point of near foundering. This is the test of all tests, the challenge of all challenges, and once conquered, it awards the spoils of an everlasting love, the bonds of which can never be broken.

The Deep Winter came to Ralph and me one bright and beautiful morning when we least expected it. With my coffee cup in hand and slippers on my feet, I moseyed out to the barn to do the feeding, like it was any other morning. Little did I know that on this day Ralph would test me as never before.

I had his bucket of oats in one hand and his flake of hay in the other. As I approached my twelve-hundred-pound friend, he faced off with me with the strength of a lion in his eyes. I wasn't prepared to handle his challenge wearing house slippers and a robe. I hadn't a crop or whip in hand to fend him off, only a useless coffee cup with less than an ounce of lukewarm liquid in it. There was no halter or rope within reach to contain him.

I wanted to run, but I knew there wasn't enough time to get away from what he was about to do to me. As the seconds ticked by in slow motion, the way they do when danger is imminent, I saw full well the message his eyes of fire were delivering to me. And I knew neither a crop, a rope, nor a halter would be enough to protect me from his challenge. I needed something much stronger, farther reaching, more powerful, and he wasn't about to give me time or space to gather my wits.

I tried to look away like they tell you to do when a bear is on the attack, hoping he'd change his mind. I tried to pretend I didn't understand his resolve, but he knew I was pretending, so he forged ahead with his assault. If Ralph and I had learned nothing else, we'd learned to read one another like a book, therefore he was relentless in this, his most powerful move to date. He stared into my eyes and with one look, he demanded I listen. With that one look he asked me to do for him what he couldn't do for himself. He asked me to stop his suffering, to kill the pain. To let him go.

I approached, and he didn't step forward to greet me. He couldn't. I lifted the bucket of oats to his mouth, and he refused my offer. I set the flake of hay near his feet, and he could not take the step necessary to find nourishment. I wrapped my arms around his neck and placed my hand over his heart. It was beating faster than normal to cope with the discomfort, and his chest was damp with sweat. I didn't need a doctor to tell me what was happening. Ralph was more than capable of explaining every last detail of where we were. We were facing our Deep Winter, and I owed it to him not only to believe him but to honor his request.

I called the vet, and after he examined Ralph, he told me what I already knew. He asked me if I wanted to wait a few days to think it over, and I said, "No. It's time for rest."

I walked over to Ralph and placed his halter on his head for the last time. It took all the strength the two of us could muster to walk, step by painful step, out to the roadside. We took it slow. It was time to let go, but neither of us was in a hurry to get there. The doctor gave me a few minutes to say good-bye. I placed my forehead against Ralph's and looked into his brown-black eyes one last time. I tried to still my pounding heart, but just like on the day we first met, I couldn't. So this time I dropped my guard at his feet.

I balanced on my tiptoes and whispered into his ear, "Thank you for teaching me to stand up for myself, to draw lines and boundaries in the sands of life, and to turn fear into anger, anger into courage, and courage into love. Thank you for being the most honest friend I've ever known and for showing me what a relationship with God looks like." Then I said what Ralph longed to hear, the words that brought life and love and so much happiness to his broken, rebellious heart so long ago: "You are such a good boy, Ralph. Such a *good* boy."

Fortuity was kind to us that day. A soft summer breeze blew and carried with it shards of leaves, earth, and destiny that bit our necks, forearms, and faces. He closed his eyes and a single tear fell short of washing the sting away. He was asking for my hand, so I—without hesitation or foresight of consequence—leaned in to him and brushed away the pain. He opened his eyes and out poured nothing less than deep love and gratitude.

That was the last time I touched Ralph and the last time I was close enough to memorize the sweet smell of his skin, a smell that to this day remains etched in my memory . . . that of lavender, dandelion, and wild mint leaves.

Chapter 8

WOMEN AND ROSES
untangling the knot around self-worth

Year: 2005 / **Age:** 50
Place: my rose garden

t first all I could hear were the birds in the trees all around me, too many to count, and the trickling of water flowing, satisfying my thirsty friends. My fifty-year-old knees were screaming bloody murder, and as usual I told them to hush up, and as usual they ignored me. It was all I could do to crouch down and hold the hose at the base of each shrub, but I learned long ago that wet foliage burns in the sun and allows mold to grow overnight. So I endured the pain in order to do what was best for them. My roses, that is.

That's love. Crouching in ninety-degree heat, bleeding from the backs of your hands and fingers to make certain they grow up happy and healthy. My roses have always thanked me for it. The minute their thirsty roots feel the cool, clear water, they call up to me loudly and clearly with the sweet scents of Audrey Hepburn, Mr. Lincoln, and my favorite rose of all: Belle Doria. By the time I'm finished weeding, pruning, and spraying the mold-B-gone, my knees may be killing me, but my roses are as pretty as any blue-ribbon winner at the county fair. My reward this day was, as always, gorgeous stems piled high on my porch, enough to fill every vase in the house.

As the hot sun bore down on my bare shoulders, the Lord whispered, *You are My rose, Michele.* He caught me completely off guard, probably because I didn't much feel like good company for anyone, especially God. I'd been down in the dumps for days, feeling like life was passing me by.

The calendar was more sparse than I'm comfortable with. It had lots of blank squares on the pages. I hate blank squares. I don't like admitting it, but an empty calendar makes me feel worthless. In my book, the more squares filled, the better.

When I was almost done watering, a cardinal sang its song into the trees. God repeated Himself. *You are My rose.*

I shrugged my burning shoulders and realized only then how depressed I was—so depressed God sounded faint and lifeless to me. "I get it, Lord, it's like the parable of the seed, and it grows with care and love like my relationship with You. And blah, blah, blah."

Yes, very true, but did you ever notice the differences as well as the similarities between your roses and Mine?

Now He had me. *Hmm,* I thought. "Ah, no. I can't say that I have," I answered and relaxed my shoulders several inches.

Then quiet. My roses were as still as night. The only sound was the trickle of water streaming from the hose.

I created women and roses much alike—soft, beautiful, unique unto themselves and each with their own sweet fragrance that brings joy to those around them. This should have delivered encouragement to my heavy heart, but all I could think of was the stick-in-the-mud I'd been lately to everyone around me.

I prune you, just like you prune your roses, Michele, especially when you're bold with blooms. I make certain that the glorious, fruitful events in your life are snipped back just so. I know this baffles you, even frustrates you, at times. He had my full attention. I had to listen closely just to keep up.

This humbles you, He continued. *You're much more beautiful and gracious this way. Just when those around you look to admire the blossoms, you look to see they're gone. I've snipped them away, but I don't throw them away, Michele. Would you like to know what I do with them?*

I was standing right in front of my Audrey Hepburn shrub, the most gracious in the garden. My blade was poised, ready to snip one of her long stems with a spotless rose on the end of it, perfect for my kitchen table. "Where do You put my blooms, Lord?"

He didn't answer me, but He did continue. *When you feed your plants, you wear gloves that allow you to reach around the thorny branches. I don't need to wear them when I feed you.*

I smiled. The thought of God wearing gloves made me want to laugh, but I said nothing and waited to hear more.

Your barbs of defense, denial, and blind spots, the very humanness covering your stems—these don't cut My hands or make Me bleed. Every drop of My blood has already been given, and My head once bore a crown with thorns much sharper than any of yours. I've known pain, much greater than your thorns can inflict, so I reach boldly among your thorn-filled branches to work on you, just like you do with your roses. When I hung on the cross, I wasn't merely cut but pierced through and through so that you might know Me, love Me, and I you.

Speechless, I was aware of nothing but Jesus. The sound of running water was silenced in my head and a peaceful hush overcame my surroundings. Even the breeze blowing through the trees seemed to cease in respect for the moment. The birds stopped their chatter. The quiet swallowed up every sound around me. I didn't take a step. I didn't make a move. I waited still, hoping to hear more.

He spoke to my heart again, *When you come out to work on your roses, you find them faithfully rooted where you last left them the day before. I, on the other hand, often have to track you down, even chase you down, to do My handiwork. And unlike your roses, you must give Me permission. You must ask, seek, and cooperate with Me for Me to do My best work. You must sit still long enough for the feeding, watering, and pruning to be done. But just as your roses warm your heart and fill your house with beauty, you, Michele, bring Me joy unspeakable and your fragrance fills My house. That's where I take your blooms, Michele, into My house. May I continue to cut and enjoy?*

I turned off the water, sat on the steps of my porch, and stared at my pile of roses. There were more than I could count, ready to take inside to enjoy. I held on to the moment as long as I could, but God's voice faded into the quiet.

The scent of a rose will never smell quite the same to me. This encounter changed forever the way I look at the lulls in my life. All I can see are vases of roses scattered through the house of God from people all over the world who are doing great things, eternal things. I may feel bare and without blooms today, but there are plenty more where they came from, because there's a tomorrow. And with it comes God's handiwork in my life, and thus more blooms. I'm thankful I wasn't off and away the day God spoke to me in the garden. God wants to fill blank squares on a calendar if we're watching and willing to hear what the Spirit is saying.

There isn't a day that goes by that I don't ask and hope for the Master Gardener to revisit me while watering my roses. He's never returned in the exact manner He did that day, but His words ring in my heart again and again. Oh, the glorious thought of His face pressed so close to mine as He takes in the fragrance of what He's created in my life. Cut all You'd like, God. Cut away!

Chapter 9

SAVING FACE
untangling the knot of bondage

———

Year: 2009 / **Age:** 54
Place: the Nashville women's prison, maximum security wing

*W*hen the phone rang on October 18, 2009, it gave me no indication of urgency or the bend in the road that lay ahead. It didn't ring with a different tone like the sound of a fire alarm, although I wish it had. At least that way I would have had a few more seconds to prepare myself for what I was about to hear. I'd just come in from feeding the dogs. My hair was pulled back in a three-day-old ponytail. My feet, bare and wet, were without traction, so I shuffled to the phone and caught it on the third ring. "Hello?"

"Michele?"

"Yes."

"It's Brian."

My heart sank because he didn't sound good. He sounded more than concerned. He sounded desperate.

"What did they decide, Brian?" I asked, holding my breath.

"You're going in."

I took a few seconds to take in His words. "Okay, if that's what I have to do."

My heart kicked up, and I knew there was nothing I could do about my fate but go with it. I didn't have a choice. That's the thing about prison. You're behind bars in your mind long before you enter the walls, halls, and cells. You're captive from the moment the idea of being there enters your timeline. I didn't want to go to the Southeast's largest women's correctional facility and hear the doors lock behind me. Who on Earth would?

The only time I'd been near a place like that was when I visited my sister Marilyn in juvenile hall when she was twelve. I promised myself, then and there, I'd never do anything to step foot in a prison. But we all have feet of clay. I thought about the apostle Paul. He probably didn't make prison one of his life goals. Joseph, one of the greatest men of God in history, found himself in a cell, too, and now it seemed God had similar plans for me.

I tried to sound brave. "Will someone pick me up or will you take me in?"

"I'll let you know, Michele, but you don't have much time." Brian was as sober as a judge. "You'll have to be inside by 5:00 p.m., right before evening lockdown, and you can't bring anything with you but a Bible."

"That's it? Nothing else?"

"Nothing else, Michele. I'm sorry. Those are the rules," Brian said.

I don't remember saying good-bye before hanging up the phone. He'd been telling me for weeks that it might go down this way. But right when I accepted the fact that going in was inevitable, things turned on a dime with the authorities, and

I wasn't going in. Brian called me a couple of times earlier in the week, telling me I was off the hook, and I was more than relieved.

I learned years before that God makes these big decisions, not men. So on this day, with nothing but a Bible in hand, and feeling about as ill-prepared as a person can feel for such things, I'd go to the Nashville Women's Maximum Correctional Facility and serve time with more than seven hundred women.

I should have taken a shower, but it never came to mind. Instead, I ran outside for some fresh, clean, open air. I walked to the one and only place I go when I need to hear God. I went straight to my barn. It's always the surefire conduit in times of crisis. My heart: crazy and conflicted. My palms: sweaty. My mouth: dry. But God always hears me best when my mouth is dry. I walked, pacing up and down the center aisle of my old poplar barn, asking, pleading for help.

I opened with the bottom line, "I'm scared, God." I prayed. And I walked some more. "I don't know how to do this. Are you sure I have to do this?" I knew the answer to that question before I asked it.

"Stay on task, Michele. You haven't much time," I reminded myself.

"You alone, God, know each girl there. You alone know how she's wired. You know what she needs. I don't. You know what I need to bring," I said and paced a new groove in the hardwoods like an expectant father mars the hospital tiles.

Tell them they're loved. God's voice spoke loud and clear, straight into my heart.

Then walking, walking. "That's it?" I asked, and then more walking, walking, walking. But nothing, nothing, nothing. "Um. Excuse me, but I'm speaking for an hour, and I have to leave in forty-five minutes! I'd appreciate a little more than, 'They are loved'!"

More walking, walking, walking.

He continued, *Tell them they are enough.*

"That's nice, Lord," I said. "Could You elaborate?" More walking still.

I was hoping for more lecture notes from God, but instead He chose better for me. He carried the hearts of the inmates up and out of the prison walls and dropped them straight into mine. My heart felt heavier than lead. While at the same time I felt the essence of God's will for the women. *I want them to know that they are more than this world has convinced them they are.*

God eased back in with one last thing, *Tell them they are priceless.*

"That's beautiful, Lord," I said, hoping that flattery would prime the pump, offering me further elaboration. But, no. I kept up my endless walking, until the clock on the wall told me I was out of time.

"I have to go, Lord. Will You come with me, please? I don't know how to do this."

"You already told Him that, Michele," I reminded myself.

"Oh, yeah." I answered. (Now I was reduced to talking to myself.)

I glanced over my shoulder to see if anyone but God was listening. My horse Sunny threw me a look, letting me know he was the only other one around. I thanked my faithful friend with a pat on the rump and ran back to the house to get ready, though I don't remember much of anything after Sunny's pat. I do remember taking a minute to jot down Scripture and notes that went along with the three messages from God.

From time to time I bite off more than I can chew. That's

how I got in this giant-sized pickle. Months ago I'd told my friend Brian I'd like to go into the prison to be with the inmates. *Who am I if I only do paid gigs like women's conferences and Sunday morning services?* I wondered. But now that "going in" was a reality, I was scared speechless.

Normally, when I do what I do, people come to the event of their own volition to hear what the night will bring. Not these women. *They'll see right through anything that resembles malarkey, Michele. You better not use one word of Christianese, little girl. If it ain't 100 percent for real, they'll string you up by your thumbs.* I lectured myself all the way down the interstate.

Brian Mason is the kindhearted soul who brings people into the prison to lead the Friday night chapel meetings, and we decided to meet halfway at the Cracker Barrel parking lot. I jumped into Brian's car, and he filled me in on the finer details of leading the service.

"Okay, Michele, the tough ones sit on the back row. They only come to chapel to get out of their cells for a couple of hours. The gals who know Jesus sit in the first two rows. The rest are sprinkled around the room."

Note to self: *Don't look at the ones on the back row.*

Brian continued, "You can't ask them anything personal, like why they're in prison. You can't go one minute past 7:55 p.m. They have to be back in their cells by 8:00 p.m. sharp. If you go over, we're both in trouble and won't get asked back."

"No pressure. Got it," I said.

"Most of these gals are in here because of men," Brian said matter-of-factly.

"What do you mean?" I asked.

"Well, they either ran with a bad boy and got in trouble doing something for him or with him. Or they were abused by a man and killed him. They decided at some point that real prison was better than the one they were living in with their abusers. If they didn't have good legal representation, they wound up with a life sentence."

"Wow," was my reply, and for the first moment since the phone call, I felt a direct connection with these women. As a child I shared their plight. I'd rehearsed killing my mother in my mind on more than one occasion along the way. Listening to Brian made my fear melt into sadness and a deep love for them.

I gazed out of the passenger-side window, and let my mind drift off into the trees, flying by at seventy mph on I-65. *What if I'd murdered Mom for beating me? What if I'd had enough one day and had taken matters into my own hands?* I thought. I'm no different than these inmates, Lord. Oh, how we need You. Brian and I were quiet for most of the remainder of the drive.

The Lord spoke many things into my heart along the way, but mostly what I felt was His love for the women I had yet to lay eyes on. This love was strangely deep, newly kindled, and white-hot. It melted away my last ounce of fear. I felt relaxed feeling God's arms around me, around the girls. I felt almost sleepy as we drove along the freeway, mile after mile after expectant mile. Somehow I knew this night and everything it held belonged to God, and I simply was invited to be a part of it. God had chosen my personality, my experiences, and my voice, but He would be the One to shine tonight.

At 6:00 p.m. sharp the women filed in one by one. They were dressed in blue scrubs with white stripes down their pant legs and large black numbers stenciled across their backs. I got scared again. No surprise. Their faces told their stories. Some looked childlike but more like a lost child searching for her mother in a sea of shoppers on Christmas Eve. Some of them looked vacant, and others looked mad. The rest looked hard as nails, like they had buried their pain in a place where they'd made sure no one could ever find it. Not even God.

I stepped up to the podium and looked down at my notes. I tried to compose myself; then at the last second I decided to come clean.

"Hi."

Deathly quiet. Blank stares.

"I don't know you. And you don't know me from Adam's house cat. I've never done this before. I've never seen the inside of a prison, but you and I have more in common than you know. I could easily be sitting beside any one of you, wearing blue scrubs. I promise you we'll get into those details at some point, but there's one thing I know, and I knew it before I got here: God loves you. I felt His love for you from the minute I asked Him how to do this, how to come here, what to say to you. You may have thrown Him away the same day you threw away the creep who landed you in here. Maybe you shut God out the first time you heard your cell door slam. Or maybe you hang on to God for dear life since yours has been taken away. All I know for sure is, starting tonight, God wants to make it clear to you that He's nothing like the people you hung out with before you got here. In fact, He's nothing like anyone you've ever known."

Tiny smiles started popping up all around the room. Not along the back row, mind you, but every other row was listening.

I told them how I'd had but forty-five minutes to prepare for the evening. "When I need to hear from God in a hurry, there's only one surefire place in the whole world I know to find Him: in my barn," I said, and the women laughed for the first time.

One by one, I told them the three things God wanted them to know.

"Tell them they are loved." And then I told them my reply. "Is that it, Lord?"

I paced back and forth along the front of the chapel floor, improv-style, using my hands, feet, and face to reenact what happened in my barn hours earlier. I told them how scared I was, and how the longer I walked, the more God's love for them carried me away from my fear.

"God understands your view of men. And of fathers."

I told them stories of my life, of hiding under beds and having a father who said he loved me but then never came around. I told them about the kind of men I dated before God showed me what I'm worth. But mostly, I kept repeating the three things He wanted them to know: *You are loved, you are enough, and you are priceless.* It wasn't my place to question these messages, only to walk them into the girls behind razor wire. And as God's words touched and fed the inmates, they touched me too.

I took them into the Bible text where Jesus said that He didn't come to bring peace but a sword.[1] Those most unexpected words from the mouth of God perked up the ears along the back row, just as they did mine when I first read them. I went on to read the rest of the passage: "He uses the sword [and I held up my Bible] to slice through and separate us from the things we've learned from our mothers and fathers, and He replaces it all with His character, His love, His perfect authority." I assured them that even though behind bars, they held the power to bring deliverance to their children. "The power of prayer can break the same curses, character traits, and addictions that landed you in here. Fight on your knees, ladies. Fight on your knees."

When I saw that time was getting short, I asked them to do something that scared me more than it scared them. I asked them to stand, one at a time, and speak out about whatever it was they wanted Jesus to sever from their lives.

"What have these things cost you? How much of a liability have these flaws become in your life? And what two traits would you want God to give you instead?"

I pointed at a woman in the front row and prayed she would stand up. She did, and she spoke clearly and with purpose. Her name was Jan. "I don't want to hurt anymore. I hurt so bad. I hurt so deep. I want to be happy. I want to know real joy. I want to laugh again." She eked out each word through a river of tears.

Every one of us was looking at a five-foot-three-inch sculpture of pure pain. Her face was contorted, twisted, knotted, and etched with deep crevasses of bottomless misery. Her windshield was pitted with divots and dings from too many miles traveling at speeds far above the maximum limit. Was she the driver or the passenger? I didn't know, but I'd never seen anything like it in all my life. Looking at Jan was like witnessing a horrible traffic accident. I wanted to look away, but I was there to do a job, and this was part of it. Pacing my barn aisle in no way prepared me for her image. Yet, if God somehow had shown me Jan's face ahead of time, I wouldn't have come. How I'd overlooked it 'til now was beyond me. I knew it would be days, months, or maybe never before the snapshot of Jan's face would fade from my memory.

Jan's face today wasn't the one God intended her to wear. The face He'd created was long gone. All that remained now was the deformity that comes via reprehensible sins. Horrible things had been done to her. I was certain of this. She was now imprisoned by those experiences, encased in them more than in these prison walls. As I stood before her, I doubted whether the sword of Christ could cut through and separate Jan from the deeds of her lineage. I was certain and ashamed of myself for my utter disbelief. But in my heart of hearts, I believed only death could free Jan from the violations her face portrayed.

The girl sitting next to Jan stood up and put her arm around her and spoke her own confession. "I don't want to hate myself anymore. I want to respect myself one day. I want to respect someone, anyone."

The next inmate stood. "I don't want to die. I don't want to die. I want to live."

And the next. "I don't want to worry about my kids. I want to feel peace so I can sleep at night."

Right down the line. "I don't want to keep killing him in my mind over and over again. I want to learn how to forgive him. I need forgiveness."

Each voice, each request ushered in the Holy Spirit to move within that particular woman. When everyone was standing except for the back row, I held my breath and motioned to the first girl on the back row to stand. The whole row stood up together in unison, and they didn't look happy. *Oh, my Lord. What are they going to do now?* I wondered. The armed guard took a step toward them.

One by one, each woman along the back said what she needed from God. I can't remember their words. I wish I could, because they were the most powerful of all previously spoken. Their words were steel-cut honest. Foul spirits and ancient curses wrapped in razor wire and cinder block were no match for God. As their confessions hit the air from out of the darkness, the Light of lights did as He promised, convincing each woman that things could be different. When the back row finished, I asked everyone to sit down.

"Let's pray." We began surrendering everything we'd asked for. In midsentence, just as I was about to say *Amen*, I remembered my dream and seeing my baby son in heaven.

I stopped praying. "Ladies, I'd like to tell you why you and I are so very much alike. Like some of you, I have taken a human life, only I wasn't arrested for it. I wasn't forced to stand in front of a jury of my peers, but I have served time for it in my own inner hell." I told them about my abortion, and that's when the last remnant of resistance came tumbling down, even along the back row. The women passed boxes of Kleenex around the room, and God's Spirit collected and bottled every tear. By this time, I was able to look every girl straight in the eye and say, "God has our babies, ladies. Now He wants us. Now He wants the mamas. No one knows better than God how it feels to lose a child, an innocent child at that. That's how He paid for your children, how He paid for mine, and that is how He paid for us. He paid with the life of His only begotten Son, Jesus, and you'll have to surrender your life to Him in order to see your children again."

I finished the prayer I'd started, and the women stood in silence and began to file out.

After the service, Jan approached me. When she got close, I couldn't look. Her face was so contorted, so deformed. She buried it in my chest and cried like a baby. "I hurt, I hurt, I hurt," she said again and again. I was at a loss for words, but we prayed just the same, and God allowed me to feel her pain. As He did, my own face began to twist and contort in empathy. We weren't quite done praying when the guard grabbed Jan by the arm. "It's time to go!" he said and dragged her wilted body out the door.

"Please pray for me, Michele," Jan pleaded.

"I will, Jan. I will. I promise I will."

Three months later I came back to the prison to conduct the Friday night chapel service again. I entered the room and immediately started scanning it for Jan. A pretty young girl ran up to me, threw her arms around me, and began talking a mile a minute about all that was going on in her life. She rattled off a long list of Scripture verses and everything God was doing for her. I tried to be polite, but I was irritated by my unsuccessful search for Jan. It was impossible to both listen and look around the room. The girl was talking so fast and loud, it was like a magnet for other women to approach the podium. They followed her lead and jumped in with their own stories and testimonies. Now I was getting really aggravated. I was so hoping to see Jan and wondered what on earth had happened to her. I did my best to answer the questions being thrown at me about what songs I might be singing that night and jotted down their prayer requests on the backside of my set list, saying, "Ah huh. Okay. That's nice," but all the while I was looking over their heads, trying to find Jan.

"Oh. Michele? Michele?" One girl tugged on my sleeve so hard it exposed my bare shoulder. "Please pray for my brother. He so needs Jesus!" the numbered lady in blue said.

I wrote down her brother's name and assured her we'd all pray for him. The other inmates at the podium chimed in with more prayer requests, and I wrote as fast as I could, hoping not to miss any of them. The service went well, but I never saw Jan. I did my job with her face in the back of my mind the whole time. The night came and went without her. I wanted to ask the other women what happened to Jan, but the prison rules didn't allow that. I left the prison that night with a deep sadness in my heart. When I got home I said one final prayer for Jan before I fell asleep.

The next morning at 6:00 sharp I sat straight up in bed from a dead sleep and slapped myself on the forehead. "That was Jan!" I said out loud. "That was Jan!"

Oh, my gosh. Oh. My. Gosh! That was Jan who came up to me before the service started! She was the girl who went on and on about everything God was doing for her and wanted me to pray for her brother! I didn't even recognize her. Her face looked entirely different. I didn't know it was the same person!

I stumbled to the kitchen and made the coffee, shaking my head the entire time.

It had taken my brain twelve hours, eight of which I slept through, to process all that God had done for Jan since last we'd seen each other. She was new. She was as bright as the morning sun, and she didn't hurt any longer, not one little bit. She was a bundle of pure joy. She was beautiful. A lifetime of damage had been cut away and replaced by everything she'd asked God for three months earlier. Jan now bore her God-given face. The best plastic surgeon in town couldn't have done a better job. I'll probably never know the whole story this side of heaven, but her face told me the *Reader's Digest* version. Where once it was contorted and tight, twisted up like a knot, it was now relaxed and so beautiful—so beautiful, I didn't recognize her.

I've been back to the Nashville Women's Correctional Facility numerous times since October 18, 2009. They have allowed me to go into every cell block, including death row. I've told each woman there about my dream, my lost son, and about the death and resurrection of God's only Son. God uses the story of my abortion more than any other to make women thirsty for heaven. We talk about family ties and ancient roots, and watch God cut them in two. And, because she gave me permission to, I tell the inmates about Jan. Her transformation transforms women every single time. Jan's testimony is irrefutable. I'd like to think it's because one October evening God handed her back the threads of her life and whispered into her heart that she is loved, she is enough, and she is priceless. And for the first time, she believed Him. And therein lies the untangling of Jan. God started with her face, and they'll keep on untangling from there!

Chapter 10

THAT'S WHY I NEED HER
untangling the knot around my sisterhood

———

Year: 2004 / **Age:** 49
Place: Whole Foods Market, produce department

I wasn't dressed appropriately for the big occasion. How could I have been? The Host didn't send me a personal invitation to this surprise party and wasn't expecting an RSVP. His only challenge was getting me there and making sure I'd be on time. That's always the tricky part about a soirée like this. But it was nothing for Him—He has amazing social skills and endless connections.

I awoke that morning with a long list of things to do in front of me, a list of everyday things that must be done but are easily forgettable. I threw on a moth-eaten T-shirt, a pair of Levi's 501 button-fly jeans with a rip in the hip pocket, and old tennies covered with tiny paint splatters from some home improvement project long ago.

My first stop would be Whole Foods Market, then Kroger, then Target. I'd put off these errands so long, we were forced to eat eggs on toast for dinner the night before. Equipped with two extra-large insulated grocery bags, I dislodged a shopping cart from the pile and fished out my shopping list. It got hung on the hole in my back pocket and ripped in two. The smaller half floated to the floor. I bent over to pick up the scrap and tripped the electric eye on the auto-open doors with my hind end. A rush of cool wind caught the slip of paper, and I took off after it as if chasing a disobedient child. The only thing keeping my runaway list from skipping all the way back to Ben and Jerry's was that it got lodged in the spokes of an antique produce cart on Aisle 1.

It's gonna be one of those days, I thought and shook my head.

I rolled my buggy up to the adorable display of oranges and plucked my list from its spokes, and that old familiar smell mowed me over. They say that of all the senses, smell stays locked in the memory banks the longest and can pull you back to its origin in an instant. I believe that, 'cause as I stood over the dimpled beauties, piecing my list together, their smell carried me back to 1960.

For the first six years of my life I grew up surrounded by oranges. We lived in the smaller of two farmhouses on my Gran-Pa's farm in Garden Grove, California, when Garden Grove was still gardens and groves. My sisters and I ran around the trees butt-naked most every day. Who needed clothes? It was seventy-five degrees all year long, and the closest neighboring farm was two miles away. Sometimes Mom made us wear shoes to avoid trips to the ER, but that was about it. Before dinner, she lined us up like planks on a picket fence and hosed us off before allowing us inside. We loved the freedom, and she loved a light laundry basket.

We climbed every tree in those orchards at one time or another and asked Mom for sugar to build ant farms in the mounds of soft, black dirt surrounding the trees. We had rotten orange fights with one another and with an occasional neighbor kid, but after being out-thrown by Madeline and Marilyn, they never came back for round two. Nothing stings like getting nailed in the butt with a rotten orange. That was my first life lesson: "Never turn and run! Face your fears to save your hiney!"

But since I was the youngest kid with the weakest arm, most times I opted for hiding behind a nearby tree, quiet as a field mouse until the coast was clear. Madeline and Marilyn could out-throw any boy within a five-mile radius. The only downside to these encounters was that we had to get dressed. But it was worth it. By the time my sisters got done with those rough-and-tumble farm boys, we enjoyed the reward of watching them run away home, crying like little girls, dappled with bruises from head to toe! No one had a stronger arm than Madeline.

Living on the farm made us brave, assertive, and, for the most part, healthy. We drank fresh-squeezed orange juice—as much as we wanted—all day every day. Later, when we moved to the city, Mom tried to pawn off frozen OJ on us one morning. We spat it out in unison. It went over just about as well as wearing clothing did.

When I awoke from my trek down memory lane, I was standing somewhere between the oranges at Whole Foods Market and the ones from my childhood. I tore off a plastic produce bag and spent the next two minutes trying to figure out how to open it. I reached for a fat, juicy orange when the woman next to me reached for the same one.

"You go ahead," I told her.

"Ah, that's okay, it's yours," she answered back, with a smile.

We both looked into the other one's eyes, and it hit me: she and I were friends. Neither knew the other's name, where

_ other came from, or what we each did for a living. I didn't know her shoe size or her favorite color. Children, no children? Who knew? What we'd had for breakfast? Who cared? On a diet? Probably not. Happy with our husbands? Whatever. Was her home larger than mine? That was a no-brainer, because I was living in a singlewide, nine-hundred-square-foot trailer and wasn't apt to move in the near future. I didn't know her phone number. I didn't know her height or weight, nor did I care to. Was the diamond on her left hand bigger than mine? It may have been, but I didn't notice.

All I remember is that we dove into each other's souls with a single glance, and we both felt a sisterhood, a connection that was real, palpable, and eternal. We needed each another. We respected each other. And best of all, we were finally able to feel the fireworks of our communion, because we were comfortable in our own skins. I can't remember who bagged the biggest orange. It didn't matter, because we were both willing to let the other pick and choose at will.

So, this is how it feels to be grown-up. This is what grown-up, whole women do. They listen. They wait. They stop in time. They breathe. They let it go. They don't hang on to what they can't control. They're free. They know there's plenty to go around. They are untangled. These thoughts and more flooded my heart. *Wow. What a deal. When did my womanhood marinate and come to fruition? When did this secure, grown-up feeling become my own?*

I wasn't sure, but I was certain that this was the day of my Bat Mitzvah, wearing T-shirt, speckled tennies, and all, and in the most unlikely of places: the produce department of Whole Foods. I wanted to ask her if this was her big day as well. Or was hers yesterday, the day before, last week, or maybe even five or so years ago?

I was a far cry from the girl who lived through June 12, 1968. That day I stood on the girls' side of the gym at the junior high dance, waiting to be asked. Waiting and waiting for the boy who would never come for me. I was the only girl in the whole school left standing alone, song after miserable song. I was reduced to hoping Claude Burns, the biggest nerd in the eighth grade, would dance with me. But no! He was busy dancing with the biggest nerdette in the eighth grade, and I envied her for it. And what did that make me? Below nerdiness. Sub-nerddom was all I could reckon.

I stood frozen, sweating like an ice cube in the summer sun, wearing my tartan skirt and fishnet panty hose. Somewhere around song number nine, I realized the full severity of the situation. I unlocked my knees and ran to the girls' restroom in a panic. I sat locked in a stall, on a toilet seat lid for fifteen minutes, tending my status wounds. Should I go home? Or, maybe another application of Revlon's White Frost lipstick would help? I searched for answers. I'm just too tall! That's it! That's my problem! Nope, it's that I'm as flat as a board! That must be the reason. I balled up a wad of toilet paper and stuffed it into my AA bra when the light went off. *This'll never work. If it's a slow dance, my boobs will feel like yesterday's biscuits,* I feared. And it echoed around the room in agreement. I tossed the wad into the toilet and watched it sink like a stone.

The muffled DJ's voice called for "Last dance. Girls' choice." I pulled myself up by my patent leather go-go bootstraps and headed for the boys' side of the dance floor with a sense of clarity and purpose. I made a beeline for Tim, the only boy in school taller than me. I'd had a crush on him all year and felt certain I'd just cracked the case of the nondancing girl. Confidence. *I just need to act confident!* I said to myself. But when the other boys saw me coming, they split and backed up like the parting of the Red Sea to get out of my way. Tim stood pinned against the gym wall with nowhere to go, like a buck in the headlights.

"Hey, Tim." I glanced down at my AAs wishing I'd gone for the toilet paper trick. When I looked back up at Tim, he was looking at them, too, lackluster. "Ya wanna dance with me?" I asked.

He said yes, but I don't think he really wanted to.

The 45 rpm recording of "Hey Jude" by the Beatles is seven minutes and seven seconds long, but to Tim it probably felt like seven hours. The naw, naw-naw-na-na-na-naws elicit cramping in all major muscle groups when you're trying your best to avoid all bodily contact.

But today was not that day.

It also wasn't July 26, 1970, when I went to the drive-in movie theater on my fifteenth birthday with John Kelley and felt his hands where hands had never gone before and hadn't the slightest idea of how to stop them.

And it was not August 1 of that same year when Jeff Noon asked me to hop on the back of his motorcycle on a Saturday night and drove 100 mph down Westminster Boulevard wearing nothing but shorts, a tank top, and flip-flops. My hair blew wild in the wind, nary a helmet in sight. I wrapped my arms around his rock-hard abs, praying my knight wouldn't land us both in a body bag.

No, today was not August 1 or July 26, 1970.

I'd survived all the way up to 2004 and had become the woman God intended me to be: untangled from the sleeping pills; untethered from the grief of the county clinic; forgiven of adultery, divorce, and all that followed. I'd lived to forgive my mother, my father, and my family in general, and I'd learned to trust God's forgiveness. Unafraid to speak my mind. Unafraid of getting old. Knot after knot, untangled. I was the woman God so loved, the woman He died to save.

And, Lord? Who is this woman beside me, filling up her own bag of oranges? Her eyes told me she was untangled too. God had somehow freed her as well. We were free from every magazine ad that told us we weren't beautiful enough, every TV commercial that made us feel small, fat, unimportant, and boring. Free from every fad diet, and the dread of wrinkles. Free to stop shopping. Free from boys on bikes and husbands who hit us. These things and people were in the past on this day in 2004. We were free from comparison. Free from competition. Free. Free. Free. Right there in Whole Foods with all the oranges cheering us on!

We chitchatted about this and that. We bagged more oranges than either of us cared to buy. We laughed for real and allowed lulls of silence to fill the empty spaces. Then we said our good-byes that seemed more like see-you-laters. I pushed my shopping cart away and felt sad that I didn't know her better, that we were out of time—for now.

God said, *You'll see her again.* I smiled.

"Have a great day," I called back to her.

"You too," she replied.

"Have a great rest of your life, and I know you will, because you're resting in God and nothing else." That's what I wanted to say to her. "Who knows what it cost you to get there? Who knows what storms you've suffered through to find out that God is more powerful than any one of them," I wanted to say, too, along with "I'm with ya, Girl. I've been there, done that. We made it! With God, we made it." I said this to myself and to her as I drifted over to the coffee aisle.

On the drive home, I asked God more about what He meant

when He told me I'd see her again. I assumed He was referring to heaven, but I'd learned long ago never to assume anything about what God says. *You'll grow old with her, Michele, or someone just like her. You'll sit in a home together, playing cards and laughing about the crazy things you did for your husbands to make them feel like men. You'll rag on them, up one side and down the other, just to keep from crying, and will admit that you'd pay any amount of money to have one more miserable day with those silly men of yours. You'll help each other to your rooms each night and pray together before you close your eyes. You'll ask Me to carry you home together, knowing full well the unlikelihood of that, for I denied you that hope when I took your husbands home. But if I do take you together, you'll leave this earth holding tight to one another's hands, just like you did in kindergarten, before you learned to be careful about such things, before you felt the need to hold hands with boys and jobs and children. That's who she is, Michele. She'll be the last one standing with you, for you, for Me. That's why you love her. That's why you need her, because you'll need her even more later on.*

I don't remember the rest of the drive home, how many green lights I caught or if the traffic was heavy or not. I only remember her eyes, the smell of oranges, and what the Lord explained to me.

That day, the untangled strings of womanhood became treasures, too many to count. But three of them are contentment, peace, and freedom. Freedom to see and celebrate beauty in the women around me. And the freedom to see my own beauty, finally. A freedom that comes only from time spent with Jesus, the Beautiful One, from whom I have inherited my eyes, ears, and smile. My dad's cheekbones only serve to hold them all together.

Chapter 11

LIVING IN THE LAND OF OS
untangling the knot around my creation

———

Year: 2012 / **Age:** 57
Place: my barn

got up, threw on a pair of jeans, and pulled my hair back in a knot. I didn't bother brushing my teeth. That's something we all do and never admit to—waiting until noon to brush. What was the point? I'd have worse things than plaque in my teeth before long. As I made my way out to my sorely neglected barn I couldn't feel anything but my rubber boots hitting the backs of my calves. I take that back. My forehead was freezing and my fingertips were slowly going numb. It was all December's fault. She brings with her mixed precipitation here in Tennessee, and she's famous for it. She can't make up her mind about what she wants to do.

I understand her dilemma. I can't either. Do I move forward or sit on the couch another three days in my flannel PJs and a robe? Do I pray or do I do? Or, do I pray for what to do? The thing that makes it worse is having too many opinions arguing in my head. Most times the loudest one is the voice of fear or the naggings of Plain Jane feeling sorry for herself. I think Jane and cold December days are cousins. Once their voices start yakking at me it's hard to do anything but sit around and listen to them.

The fog outside was as thick as pea soup. The fog inside of me was thicker. Joe from Bonnie's Feed Store would be in at noon, and I needed to clear a spot for the delivery. Truth is, my get-up-and-go got up and went somewhere and I wasn't sure why. Sometimes those are the hardest blues to kick, the ones you can't put your finger on. A fresh start is what I needed. But if there's one thing I've learned, it's that fresh starts don't just happen, they take work. When I'm feeling lifeless to the bone, an encounter with the living God always works to kick-start me back to life, and many times those heavenly encounters happen in my barn.

If anyone knows God has not abandoned them, it's me. I've seen Him make a way when there was no way, give me life for death, and buy back my soul when I'd already sold it for a lesser price. He has dealt gently and graciously after my many end-over-end tumbles down life's mountaintops and hillsides. But even so, it's never easy to sit and wait to hear God's still, small voice, especially when I am anxious, fearful, or really hurting inside. The sinking feeling we all experience in prayer—waiting, waiting, waiting—is yet another thing few of us ever admit to. Most times I cop out and just call a friend for advice or I clean the house or just worry more. When I do take the time to sit and ask for God's help, I begin with praise. If I don't start that way I suffer from amnesia, completely forgetting about the countless prayers He's already answered and then I wonder why my words boomerang off the ceiling.

"Lord, can You hear me?" I prayed out loud and watched my

words disappear into the dense fog. "I need clarity, Father." When I'm feeling this blue, my prayers are not vague. If I've learned one thing, it's that God is not impressed with lofty, wishy-washy prayers. If I want Him to be specific with His answers, I have to be specific with my questions. And if my prayers are draped in unbelief, I might as well not bother praying at all.

"I need to talk *with* You, Lord. Not just *to* You," I said. "I'm grateful for all You've done for me. You've taught me to ask and expect to be heard, so here I am, Father." With that said, mindless, random thoughts entered my prayer space with ideas like, *Don't forget to call Cindy before noon* and *What's for dinner tonight?* These distractions pull me away from the throne of God more times than I care to admit to. I think that's how we all drift away from God. It happens just one mindless diversion at a time.

The last straw was when my nose started running like a faucet. "Perfect!" I said, and wiped my nose with the back of my glove and gave up trying to hear from my invisible God.

But, then, there He was.

He wasn't audible. The roof of my barn didn't levitate or shake. The wooden shutters didn't flap or slam shut, yet His presence was powerful. It was similar to the night I sensed Jesus beside me on my bed when the enemy was trying to push me into an early grave, only this time I wasn't startled by God at all. Knowing that the Father is near enough to touch is familiar to me now. I didn't know how to "be" with God the Father in 1985. In fact, I didn't know how to spiritually tackle His absence in my life until I was in my forties. My perception of the Father was of alien nature. But He changed all that when I got sick and tired of living with the huge father-shaped hole in my heart.

Now when He's near, my heart settles and I breathe Him in and relax in who we are together. I don't sit up straight as if there's a yardstick glued to my shoulders. He is the Father to the fatherless and simply put, He loves me because I am His daughter and that's all there is to it. I know His voice. And when I hear Him speak to my heart, I don't need to rub my eyes and question my sanity or the validity of the moment as I did in 1985.

The Father spoke to me slowly and in a steady rhythm so that I could take in every word. *I AM yours, and you are Mine.*

Years ago, the great "I AM" frightened me, but I never spoke a word of this to anyone. Scripture has since taught me that the great I AM and Jesus speak the same love language. The great I AM *can* and *has* walked with me through barns, has whispered to me while I fold laundry, and has chatted with me in my rose garden. Jesus said it best, "I and the Father are one" and "If you've seen Me, you've seen the Father." Without these promises I'd still be living my life with Jesus as my Savior but not with God as my Father.

If you do the math, that is like knowing only two-thirds of God, counting the Holy Spirit, of course. If the great I AM is a stranger to you, too, you're missing out like I once was. Before I was in full relationship with all three, I felt powerless, out of place even though I was a surrendered, saved, forgiven follower of Christ.

Is God the Father holy or friend? Both or neither? Jesus' disciples had a difficult time with these questions, as did the Pharisees. God became a man to die for us but also to paint a very clear picture of how God the Father wants to be seen, felt, and known. I think it's one of the main reasons Jesus was not crucified as an infant or sacrificed while still a young man. This great I AM took on the role of a servant in Jesus. He walked the earth long enough to show us the Father. He made Himself touchable and *very* relational. With the washing of feet, cuddling innocent children, and healing sinners on the Sabbath He showed me there's no need to fear Him, in the negative sense of the word. These over-the-top bold expressions of intimacy and humble service from Jesus are healing for someone like me who didn't have a dad. Jesus broke rule after rule, law after law, making the Father accessible anytime, anywhere, on any day of the week.

Why is it that two thousand years later we still have difficulty grasping an intimate relationship with God the Father? Maybe because most of us grew up without a loving relationship with an earthly father, and that alone creates a huge hurdle to overcome. If our earthly father treated us harshly or, like mine, was an absentee dad, we fall into the trap of trying to earn God's love and acceptance. Or without knowing it we may even transfer our anger toward our dads to God.

And then there's the dichotomy between the God of the Old Testament and Jesus. At first glance, the strong hand of God in Genesis appears to be the antithesis of Jesus in the Gospels. If we never take the time to deconstruct our roadblocks to the Father's love, whatever they might be, we'll never be comfortable with Him. If that happens, we'll never be comfortable, period. We'll never know who we are or Whose we are, and we will feel like spiritual orphans.

At the assurance of Jesus' prodding, I gave myself permission to seek and know His Father just like He does, and that includes hearing the Father's voice like He did. Jesus said, "Therefore, whatever I speak is just what the Father tells Me to speak."

I laugh with the Father, because He laughs in Scripture. I cry with Him because He wept over Israel. And when I look at my life's journey, I see that the minute I dove headlong into this privilege I became secure with who I am as a woman. I finally felt safe and protected in ways I had not before knowing Him in this deep way. I stopped compromising myself in relationships. I was no longer a human doormat. I speak up when it's called for and put a sock in it when it's time to say nothing and let it go by because I have a Father and He has my back!

Yes, it *is* the great mystery. Jesus was God, and at the same time had an intimate relationship with God the Father and together, even now, they converse so that Jesus might pray for each one of us! *And* yes, they are One. It is all the great mystery and I'm glad I can't put God in a box. This keeps me humble *and* teachable.

On this very misty morning, mysteries about *my* life were about to be demystified. As I sat in the cold and heard the Father say, *"I AM yours and you are Mine,"* I listened and my barn melted into a warm and wonderful sanctuary. God wanted to clear up the foggy beginnings of my childhood. That's what knowing the Father does. The Ancient of Days surprises us with answers to our age-old questions as we sit and give Him our ears.

My questions could be traced back to before I was born. My mother's pregnancy with me was rough, really rough. I was what you might call a "life unexpected" or, plainly put, "a mistake" in human terms. That always ate at me but I never knew what to do about it. Asking about Mom's pregnancy was taboo around our house. My mother nearly miscarried me more than once and it would have made her life much easier if she had. Hearing God's opinion about such things, fifty-plus years later, was a gift I will always cherish and never forget.

I didn't interrupt God with all this commentary. I just kept listening as He spoke to my heart:

Danger was on every side of you, Michele, but I wouldn't allow it to harm you. And oh, how the enemy wanted to. He wanted to wear you down. But he couldn't touch you; for you belong to Me.

I knew God wasn't merely telling me the truth; He was the Truth and had been, long before my heart first beat. I sat still, bouncing my feet up and down on my toes to hear my back-story straight from the One who writes all our stories. He spoke to my heart in that soothing voice of His, and—as always—my heart slowed to a steady, full rhythm. He was with me, even when I was no bigger than a peanut. I'd been asking Him for the missing puzzle pieces of my life, never dreaming He could go back this far with me. He must have known I was ready to hear it. Just like the night I prayed and was carried away in a dream to see my lost son, God can take us anywhere when He chooses to restore what's been lost or stolen.

One day, He said, *after I had just calmed you from the latest uproar, without warning, things began moving and swirling, pounding and crashing again.*

It was as if I was watching a movie. God's words came to me in pictures not sentences. As the story goes, inside my mother's womb, something was very wrong. The enemy—the dark spirit, the one God called the father of lies—was stepping up his game that very hour. And if that wasn't bad enough, humans were yelling just outside the thick layer of Mom's muscle and skin covering my cocoon. But being only four months of age and the size of a lime, I couldn't make out or understand a word they were saying. In the womb, where the beginnings of life should be calm and quiet, sacred really, often things were nothing like that for me. I always knew it in some fashion. God was now offering me more detailed understanding about my blemished beginnings.

There are no gray areas in the world of the womb, Michele, God explained. *There are only the perfection of My Voice and the betrayal of the liar. My words carry infinite love and power, and the liar's words are without value. But outside the womb, the black and white of who we are becomes blurred in the eyes of man.*

I could attest to this. Everyone I know seems to have opinions about who God is and who Satan is or whether they even exist. Boundary lines of right and wrong change daily. The pride of man tells us we're right 99 percent of the time and we rarely apologize for rubs that come our way. Many call this freedom. Some even call it wisdom.

God was telling me different. If I had understood this better at the start of my spiritual journey I would never have spent one minute arguing with the liar. It would have done me well to trust God and rebuke the liar at every crossroad. To begin each day with, "search my heart, God!" would have been optimal. But I did not. For many years I did not take God at His word and obey it. And I didn't take authority over the liar, and so he beat me up on a weekly basis. Shame was his game and I was the pawn.

Because of spiritual ignorance, I had great difficulty trusting in anyone but myself. This strong human tendency to control and see things my own way has gotten me in trouble more times than I can count. At times, I *still* listen to the liar. I feel carried away by his antics. Sometimes I grab an imaginary chair, sit down, and converse with him for hours at a time. I've been created to know and love the One called I AM. His greatness is very great but His voice is very small. He only asks that I listen carefully and trust in His Word. This request is a challenge for me, because the liar's voice is loud and obnoxious, his tactics are subtle, and I'm easily distracted by them. But what I didn't know until that day was that the liar began early on with his despicable behavior toward me. I quit my inner chitchat and listened.

Before you were born, every single time the liar came around he would pull on your life and the tiny thread you held in your hand.

"What tiny thread in my hand? I was holding a thread?" I asked twice and was sure He would explain more about it later, so I stopped and listened harder. God went on:

Peace is not dependent upon the absence of fear, trouble, or confusion. Peace is My calm in the midst of all three.

I nodded and tucked these beautiful words away in a safe place in hopes I wouldn't forget where I put them.

All you wanted around you was your mother and My peace. But that's not how it was. Spirits of chaos were there. Early in your formation, these bad spirits pushed, pulled, and poisoned you. They entered the sacred space of the womb on the poison in your mother's bloodstream. She drank the poison called "liquid spirits" willingly, and by the very nature of the name, you'd think she'd understand the danger. But she didn't. Still, all was made right later when I untangled her addiction and redeemed her to the uttermost. She left this earth forgiven of her offenses. Yet there was danger all around you every time she drank. I would that she hadn't. But it's behind us now.

God stilled my pounding heart and continued:

The liquid spirits ushered in the spirits of chaos. They walked right in when your mother left the door open. They taunted her mind. Her words got slurred, and her thoughts got angry. The spirits twisted her thinking and she wanted to give up on life, even yours. But they didn't know with whom they were dealing. A battle against Me is lost before it begins.

I shivered, but not from the cold.

Your mother made choices and not wise ones. Fueled by anger, she put herself in harm's way again and again. Then came the fighting and with that the movement, lots of movement. You couldn't hold on. Your mother ran as fast as she could to escape the danger she'd created. Her slugging and stomping weakened your hold. It looked to be the end for you. Like a tsunami, a rush of white water ripped through your mother's womb. The liar yanked hard on your thread, the part of your life that was yours to hold on to, and he snatched it from your hand! That was the first time you felt deep disappointment, the first time you felt hopelessness. The first time you felt alone was the day you lost your thread.

For just a second I thought I remembered this part. But I couldn't. Not really. I could only remember a deep sadness.

He continued without a pause. *You thought the thread was lost, but I never lost sight of its whereabouts.*

I was sill foggy about the meaning of the thread but flashed back to 1985. I saw Jesus sitting with me on my twin bed and handing me the tangled ball of string, *"your life,"* as He called it. And now I was sitting with the Father, twenty-seven years later. It all made sense.

"Even though my life is Yours, parts of it are mine to manage. Oh, how far we've come together, Lord. Because of You, because of Jesus, we've untangled so many threads the enemy had control of before I knew You," I said.

God didn't comment. He knew I understood, so He went on: *You reached out into the dark waters of the womb to retrieve your thread but your arm was too short, the waters were too rough. You watched the thread twist and fray and float away into the fluid surrounding you. For all you knew, your delicate thread, your life that you loved, was now gone. Your heart cried as you watched it tangle and twist more and more. It spun and turned about itself. It tangled around and around and into a tiny sphere, yet one too large for your hand to hold. Nevertheless, you tried again and again to grab it back, to press it close to your chest for safekeeping. But it wasn't to be. You missed it every time you tried, and you watched it disappear into the dark waters of the womb.*

"I hate that my mother drank and hate how she let the liar into our sacred space to tangle my thread! He's a thug. The thug who took my thread! I always felt lost without it and didn't know why. You gave it to me. *You* made it for me. It was the part of me You put me in charge of! It held boldness and bravery and held things like gumption and creativity. It held laughter and dreams and drive and intuition and insight and smiles, lots and lots of them. It held the knowledge of right and the fear of wrong. It held Your very best for me. And it was mine to hold on to. It was my very own part of me—"

God waited. He knew I was beginning to understand Satan and his tricks as never before.

I rambled on to God: "He robs from innocent children and keeps robbing forever if allowed to and sometimes it starts before they are born. I bet I was high on booze before my tender lips ever tasted milk. Some babies are born addicted to crack and never fully recover. Satan is cold, heartless."

I whispered into the ice-cold air and watched my breath float away. I understood about the thread and how it first got tangled. My thread held the great value of my life, everything that should have flourished and thrived but instead got tangled more and more each day until I came to know God in 1973.

"But . . . wait!" I blurted out loud. "My life-thread held the luxury of choice and respect for You and respect for myself and others. I was meant to be strong! Without my thread I felt like I was worth nothing, like I had no voice and no choice in anything that mattered at all. Without it, I felt as small as I was the day I lost it. It wasn't the liar's to take and twist but he sure felt entitled to it. He wanted from me what *he* had lost so long ago—when he turned from You, Father, and found himself in darkness with no way back. He broke Your heart, and now he wants to break mine and everyone else's. He lied to himself when he wanted more than his fair share!

"When we lie to ourselves, we are just like him. So . . . there I was, without a thread of hope. I had no hope and thought surely I had no future, no gifts. No wonder I felt twisted and broken for so long—seventeen years to be exact! And then *still* felt broken even after I met Your Son. Even then, Satan didn't stop with the lies. He told me I was broken beyond repair and would always be that way." I prayed all this to the Father, with my heart wide open, and then continued.

"I bonded with other broken people and was not attracted to God's people because I felt 'less than.' Trying to rescue myself, I rescued other broken people. None of it worked. It was all upside down. I didn't flourish with the broken ones and didn't fit alongside Christians. I was so tangled and just wanted to fit someplace. Even in Your house of worship, I felt so alone. I felt odd and tangled. I was so alone in my struggles, Lord."

I wept.

God waited, again knowing what I would ask next.

"If I lost my thread, how on earth did I find You without it?"

The Lord my God sat still and allowed the truth to seep into my soul. He tucked me under His arm and held me close, just like Jesus had in 1985. He waited. Waited for me to catch up with Him.

"You've always been with me, right? Even when I was so mixed up and tangled, right?" I asked the Father.

Was I with you? Michele, I have never taken My eyes off you. I never turned My attention away. Never. And I'd like to say for the record, you were not a mistake. Most lives come into the world unexpectedly and may look like mistakes to the people involved, but no one ever enters this world by accident. I create each person.

"May I ask? Why did Mom drink? Why did she pick fights and put me in harm's way, time and time again? Why did she beat me later?" I asked.

Hurting people hurt people. From generation to generation. It's a chain of one person taking advantage of a weaker person, who then grows up to take their turn. Hurting people often let the hurt turn to anger. Anger feels more powerful to them, less exposed. It covers the pain. None of this makes it right. And we both know it doesn't help or heal it. Neither does the drinking. I wait for them to wake up. I encourage them to give Me their pain. It breaks My heart to watch them carry it alone. And it breaks My heart to watch the damage the pain inflicts on them and on those they love.

"Mmmm," I said.

Then God made a ninety-degree turn on the story.

You woke at the sound of your mother's voice. I calmed your fear of falling through the crack known as the "os." I was the only force strong enough to hold you there. You were attached to the one and only unsafe, unstable place in the uterus: atop the opening of the cervix, known as the os.

"I couldn't even do *that* right," I said, shaking my head. "And to top it off, Mom, at age thirty-five, was running low on hormones, so her body was threatening to miscarry. We were quite the train wreck."

Sweet, Michele. You're still beating yourself up for attaching to the os. The liar convinced you, from the moment you heard about it, that you were to blame. Since then, you often take responsibility for things you shouldn't. You often blame yourself for things you have no control over. Let Me tell you something. I placed you on the os. It was My idea from the start. It was My plan for you. I wanted you to know that I AM in control of all that happens to you.

Sweet relief flooded my soul. That's the beauty of talking

to God the Father. He is good and does good. He stops the madness we dream up from the past. He clears the air so we can breathe a sigh of relief.

Landing on the os wasn't your doing—and certainly not the liar's. Yes, I had My hands full. Just the way I wanted them, full of you, Michele, holding you safe and sound to the os. As close to Me as close can be. And I wasn't a bit worried. Meanwhile, your hands were tucked in little fists—one near your mouth so you could suck your thumb, and the other one was under your chin and empty, for you had lost your thread. So, these were your great challenges: losing your thread, the threats from the liar, the os, your mother's drinking, and her tendency to bleed. Of all challenges, the most dangerous was the bleeding. Every time your mom bled, it ran right beside you and out the os, and you'd feel yourself slipping away. But I held you fast to the os every single time.

"I was Your creation. The os was Your idea. Nothing about how I entered this world was a mistake! For that, and for so much more, I love You, the One I know as the I AM, my Lord, my Friend, my Father, Protector, Savior, and so many other worthy titles," I said. And I noticed I wasn't a bit cold. "You are my God, my Father."

Calling God "my Father" made my heart flutter and fly inside my chest just as it had the very first time I felt His tug on my heart in 1973. This spiritual phenomenon feels similar to the "butterflies" that flit and flutter in the human stomach, but with much more punch. Butterflies first danced inside my belly while I rode Ferris wheels, soared down hills on shoe-skates, and especially when I first fell in love with boys. But these butterflies, the ones inside my heart at the mere mention of the God's name, were not located in my stomach. They flew through the deep chambers of my soul with the velocity and nimbus of a thousand heavenly eagles!

Once God's Spirit takes flight through the human heart, it's hard to ignore and harder still to turn away. Later, outside of the womb, I would feel His presence while kicking my heels on the hood of the Chevy as fireworks flew overhead. And yet again while hiding from my mother under my bed, and again when dozing under Dee Dee's top sheet. But I would never in my life feel about my human father as I did about my Father God. Just saying God's name, or even thinking it, made the eagles take off inside of me. Referring to my earthly father only made me feel empty and sad inside. This dichotomy made me wish they were called by different names.

It was time to hear the rest of the story. I wasn't quite sure I was ready for it, but I sat and listened for what I hoped would be a wonderful conclusion. When God speaks into my heart, He's able to impart volumes of information in mere moments of time. What's taken more than seven thousand words to convey in this chapter, God imparted to me in a blink of time:

One night, God breathed on the os, and Mother's blood flowed like a river. She cradled her tummy in the crook of her arms but could do nothing to stop the bleeding, for God had made it so. Mother pressed a dishtowel between her legs with one hand and grabbed her car keys with the other. She sped down the highway trying to save my life. It didn't look promising. God held me tight to the os and He called for the Spirit. And called yet another One, more beautiful than I could ever imagine, and He stood to the right of the Father.

We were with you, Michele, watching, taking care of you, but it was time for you to go, to live beyond the womb, to listen for Me, and watch for the butterflies that fly as eagles—the Spirit, awakening you to new life. He would lead you to the Beautiful One whose name is Jesus, and Jesus would bring you to Me to be reconciled, Michele. Until that day, I'd never be far.

From the moment you left the womb, Michele, you began to die and had no ability to stop yourself from dying. Without intervention from My Son, the Beautiful One, you would have lived a lifetime of dying. Without a thread of hope, your many gifts would never have flourished. Redemption would have escaped you and your spiritual blindness would have resulted in eternal death.

I wondered how on earth this very important intervention from God's Son was spun into motion. I no sooner wondered it, than He satisfied my curiosity.

Before you left your mother's womb, I made sure to give you a cord of love, Michele. I tied one end of the cord around your heart and held tight to the other end and began drawing you to Me. You couldn't respond to my pull the day you were born, of course. You couldn't even feel it. But over time you did, and with the watering of My Word, your intervention was in full swing. You recognized My pull and the gift of My Son's life in exchange for yours just before your eighteenth birthday.

"Aahhh. Yes. I remember it like it was yesterday," I said. "I was in my little twin bed, the one I hid under as a child when I prayed my first *real* prayer to You, saying, 'Jesus come into my heart and do whatever it is You do when You get there.' I wasn't in a church but it felt like church to me!"

God smiled. *It was a beautiful prayer that ushered in everlasting life! My Holy Spirit flew into your heart and nestled Himself there. I wrote your name in My book of life and the dying in you was extinguished!*

I understood every word of it. The sweetest knowledge comes when God has won the argument.

I placed your life's treasure in you.

"My life's treasure? What's that?"

Hold on. Let's not get ahead of ourselves here.

I said, "I wish I'd felt Your pull earlier than I did. It would have saved me from so many mistakes." I bowed my head and slumped my shoulders.

Michele, the Father spoke again, *all sorts of things impaired your spiritual eyes and ears for the first seventeen years of your life. Hormones raged throughout your young body and made you believe that boys were more important than they were. Ego stepped in and told you I was trying to rob you of happiness. Pride took over, and you forgot how to feel sorry about everything with everyone. The bad spirits took a break at this point while these human traits played havoc throughout your teenage years.*

For some, dark spirits shine through crystal balls and speak through star formations, moons, and even voices from the dead to deliver them instant gratification. These tricks work for those who want answers that require no relinquishment of the human will. The dark spirits also love to work off hungry hearts and dangle carrots like houses, money, status, accomplishments, and fame in front of those hearts. They love deeply rooted bitterness in the human heart and work well off feelings of entitlement and unforgiveness. And they convince people that certain acts can never be forgiven.

And when My children robe themselves in self-righteousness and judgment, forgetting the depth of My sacrifice for them, the darkness celebrates. All the bad spirits' tricks are designed to distract and gobble up precious time. They feed the dying with counterfeit joy hoping physical death will come before spiritual life begins, that moment when Jesus, the Beautiful One is invited into their hearts and becomes their all in all. Without My Son, the lost are lulled into spiritual sleep, and when they wake up in eternal darkness, only then do they see it was the liar who sedated them. Others rest everything upon intellect, never understanding that wisdom begins with the acknowledgment of My existence. In claiming to be wise, they have become fools.[1]

But the artifice of the liar that breaks My heart, more than any other, is when the liar pits My bride against herself.

God went silent. And I sensed the unspeakable. I felt the broken heart of God.

My heart breaks when—

He couldn't get it out. The depth of His sorrow stunned me. I listened as never before.

I'm saddened when My people, My bride—those who have been sealed in the blood of My resurrected Son—run for shelter into the arms of the liar, because of the cruelty she has suffered in the company of My people. This, Michele, breaks My heart. My wounded bride, weakened, returns back into the world from which I saved her, attempting to find help and healing, with no desire to return to the fold. Oh, the sorrow I suffer from this and My Spirit is grieved beyond human understanding.

Often My church refuses to see what they have done to push the bride members away and feel justified in their cruel behavior. The liar rejoices in this handiwork, more than any other. The ramifications of this travesty stretch far beyond what eyes can see. Many of My plans are delayed or even thwarted altogether. The worldly wise onlookers, the unbelievers, are repelled by what they see and suffer for it almost more than My bride does. And because the onlookers are still part of the dying, without eyes to discern the truth of the matter, they follow the wounded bride members into the liar's trap, and he devours them all to fulfill the wounding.

This, for now, Michele, is the father of lies' greatest triumph. But mind you, there's coming a day when I will tolerate this no longer, and on that day the liar's reign will cease. I will awaken My church with a start! The alarm of great sound will pull her to her feet! My holy fire will bring death to all deception and the bride will be refined and made strong. But as for now, these deceptions are the liar's modus operandi and must be acknowledged in order to be overcome.

The fog lifted as I cried before God. I knew as never before the Father's heart. His love is perfect, and the liar—while still allowed—will convince us all, the lost as well as the found, of as many lies as we listen to, even the cruel banishing of God's beloved. I myself was guilty of such cruel judgments and more. I bought lie after lie, until God's Spirit came to me and began the untangling.

Knowing what I know now about how complicated this entire process is, from birth to resurrection, I'm surprised God ever let me out of the womb to begin with! He could have snatched me straight up to heaven in 1955.

Michele, in 1985 when My Son met you in your darkest hour, never forget how He banished the enemy with one look, one glance. You were amazed at the tangled mess your life had become in the hands of the liar. What began as a tiny, single beautiful thread—a life of promise inside the womb—was a twisted mass of lies, hurts, blindness, discouragement, shame, and so much more. But I, the One who creates life to begin with, can untangle anything. And so we have.

There is no shame in the untangling.

I closed my eyes, and this time I was the one who spoke in a slow and steady rhythm so God and I could both absorb every word. "I am Yours. You are mine. What the liar intended for evil, You, my Lord, used for good. It was my knots, my tangles, that made me desperate for You, Your help, Your love. Without need of You, I may never have thirsted for You. Had my twin bed been a canopy, dripping with silk and lace trim . . . had my sheets been clean and dry, smelling of angels' breath, I may never have called out Your name, I may never have prayed my first prayer. The liar pushed me straight into Your arms.

"My mother, my dad, and every ridiculous blunder I've made have thrown me straight into Your heart, my Lord. And You have held me, healed me, forgiven me without hesitation, every single time. I love You, Lord, and will forever love You and thank You. And even if there were no forever at all, knowing You, Your presence, and hearing Your voice has made my life on earth worth living."

I slid off the bale of hay and dropped to my knees, removed my gloves, and set them aside. I lowered my chest to my knees and pressed my palms flat onto the dirt floor. I cried tears of thanksgiving to my living God. God spoke one last time:

Keep holding fast to the threads of your life I've given you guardianship of—your will, your thoughts, your words, gifts, reactions, decisions—oh, and begin each day just as you are now. And never stop learning of Me. Together, we have fought and always will fight against the wiles of this fallen world.

I sat back up and lifted my hands to the sky. "Your hands are right where You promised they'd be, right on top of mine, holding the threads of my life for the untangling. Whatever else I'm holding on to, what seems so important at the time, is not as important as letting go. This is my life lesson," I professed, grounded in new gratitude.

And last, but not least, is this: your life's treasure, Michele—

"Oh, yes, my life's treasure. What is it?"

It's what the enemy wanted all along. It's not something made of silver or gold. It can't be bought or earned, and it will never die. Your life's treasure is a soft and tender heart that hungers for Me, Michele. And your life's treasure is woven into every thread of your life. Without the treasure of a childlike heart, it would be better for you to have slipped through the os to begin with. Keep a guard around your tender heart, Michele, for here on earth the human heart that's fully surrendered to My love is the treasure of all treasures.

I sat still for what seemed like forever. "Lord? Lord?" I asked.

Then . . . nothing. I kicked the frost from my boots and looked straight through the open air and could almost see tomorrow's sun. Just like the clouds in the sky tell me what's to come, my body now tells me where I'll soon be going. My bones are beginning to ache and my skin wrinkles more and more with every passing day. My sight is blurred and my ears are dull. Before too long God will breathe on me one last time, just like He did on the os, and I will be born to new life where there are no dark spirits, no pushing and pulling. No dying, no trying or crying or calling for help. No lying, no lonely. No worry, no fear or pounding of feet. Only singing and dancing and kicking up praises to Jesus, the Beautiful One, and the Spirit, and, of course, the Father of Lights.

He'll carry me on to the Land of Forever where there is no need for hiding under beds, mop-topped Beatles to hold my hand, or red M&Ms to sweeten the tongue, for only Love will remain. But until that day, we'll be right here, together, untangling.

Notes

CHAPTER 1 You Can't Frighten the Dead
1 Reference to James 2:19
2 Matthew 7:23b, NKJV
3 Reference to Matthew 7:21

CHAPTER 3 The Power of Forgiveness
1 Story found in John 5
2 John 19:30
3 Referenced in Revelation 13:8 and 20:12

CHAPTER 4 Found
1 Referenced in Exodus 21:23–25 and Matthew 5:38–42

CHAPTER 5 Eating Crow and Keeping It Down
1 Referenced in Luke 9:14–17
2 Referenced in Jeremiah 8:20–22
3 Referenced in Joel 2:25
4 Referenced in Deuteronomy 30:19

CHAPTER 6 In Search of the Invisible Man
1 John 14:9
2 Referenced in 1 Corinthians 10:13
3 Referenced in Psalm 105:8
4 Jesus, in John 10:30

CHAPTER 9 Saving Face
1 Referenced in Matthew 10:34

CHAPTER 11 Living in the Land of Os
1 Author's paraphrase
2 Author's paraphrase

About the Author

The voice of Michele Pillar entered the world through Contemporary Christian Radio in 1979 when she sang "Thou Art Worthy" on *The Praise II* record for Maranatha! Music. Soon after, "Jesus What a Wonder You Are," "In Moments Like These," and many other titles were hers for the series. Next, she recorded "The Misfit" with Erick Nelson and in the mid-1980s became Sparrow Record's dominant seller with recordings *Michele Pillar*, *Reign on Me*, and *Look Who Loves You Now*, earning three Grammy Award and Dove nominations and total sales of more than 1.5 million. In 1992 Michele recorded *Love Makes All the Difference* for the Benson Company. The song "You Untangle Me"—penned by Michele and Hall of Fame Writers Allen Shamblin and Mike Reid—is featured in her latest music project, available on MichelePillar.com.

When not touring, Michele and her husband, Matt, live in Leiper's Fork, Tennessee, and enjoy time with their children and grandchildren.

MichelePillar.com
Facebook.com/MichelePillar
@Michele_Pillar

The Untangling

MICHELE PILLAR

a journey through
THE UNTANGLING

A COMPANION GUIDE FOR
UNTANGLED

A COMPANION GUIDE FOR
UNTANGLED

*Group Leader notes are included

Michele's Live Event

THE CLOTHESLINE CONFERENCE
Getting untangled from the inside out

"Michele's strongest gift, besides singing, is her ability to connect with people!"
–BEBE WINANS

As they take their seats, audiences are captivated by a full-scale clothesline, center stage. Minutes later, they are hearing Michele's signature music, laughing along with her honest stories as she hangs garments on the line with tiny wooden clothespins. Soon, a wardrobe of redemption unfolds right before everyone's eyes. God's Word and promises are intertwined, and soon, all in attendance recognize garments of their own that they've worn far too long.

"We wear and carry things God wants. He longs to dress us in His goodness, peace, forgiveness, and power! But first we have to give Him our tattered past. At the end of The Clothesline, *the Lord is right there, ready to pick up our laundry because it no longer fits, it's out of style, and the only wise choice is to leave it all behind on* The Clothesline.*"*
–Michele Pillar

Watch *The Clothesline* seven-minute promo video on:
WWW.MICHELEPILLAR.COM
The Clothesline can be your next event!
Call or email Melissa Longbrake:
Melissa@MichelePillar.com or Direct: 615-884-6417

Full-day events include complimentary note booklets

Untangled Resources

Go to MichelePillar.com to enjoy
Untangled at discounted prices. Click "Shop!"

You can also order additional copies of *Untangled*
at your favorite online retailer.

Also available is an **audio book** and **e-book**.

Michele's Music

From her CCM classics to her latest releases
(All Available on CD or Download)

You Untangle Me (2016)
Produced by: Joe Chiccarelli & Randy Younger
Title song by: Grammy Award winners,
Allen Shamblin & Mike Reid

You Untangle Me Performance Tracks
(All Titles)

I Hear Angels Calling
A Christmas CD For All Year Long

Love Makes All The Difference
(Michele's 1992 Release)

Michele's Music

Forever Young
20 Classic Favorites from the 80s & 90s

The *Found* Video
Seen by hundreds of CPC Directors,
this same video Michele has performed live, }
at CPC Banquets since 2008. A great ministry
tool for pregnancy centers.
(On CD or Download)

Sheet Music (Select Songs)
Email desired song title to:
Melissa@MichelePillar.com

For song titles on each CD, go to www.MichelePillar.com

Let's Be Social

Become a "liker" on Michele's FB Fan Page!
Click the "Like" button and receive the 2-Minute Miracle
Bible Devotional, Mon-Fri.
Michele's Page will feed your spirit and encourage your heart.
Hear her music and enjoy everyone's comments. See why her
Page reaches over 20 million people weekly.

And don't forget to check out Michele's Website!
www.MICHELEPILLAR.com

MichelePillar.com